Soccer Tough:
Simple Football Psychology Techniques to Improve Your Game

by Dan Abrahams

BENNION
KEARNY

Mum, Dad, and Heidi.

This book is not only for you, it is also because of you.

Acknowledgements

I'd like to thank these players for allowing others to learn from their soccer journey:

Shaun Batt, Carlton Cole, Anthony Stokes, Richard Keogh, Elvis Putnins, Barry Fuller, Marc Bircham, and the Gallen brothers - Kevin, Steve and Joe.

Your willingness to allow others access to your challenges, on and off the pitch, is testament to your commitment and passion to grow as footballers.

About the Author

Dan Abrahams is one of the foremost soccer psychology consultants in Europe. As a former professional golfer he holds a First Class Honors Degree in psychology and a Master's Degree in sport psychology.

Dan is a psychology consultant to QPR in the English Premier League and has worked with more than a dozen professional clubs and hundreds of players over the past 10 years. He has some of the most exciting case studies from the past decade including helping professional soccer player Carlton Cole go from forgotten reserve team player to England international.

Dan is also a speaker in demand at universities, colleges, clubs and soccer organizations. He has delivered his message to governing bodies including the English Football Association, the Professional Footballers' Association, and the League Managers' Association.

Dan has spread his soccer psychology philosophies across the soccer globe by using social media and his mindset techniques are now used by players and coaches across Europe, the USA, the Middle East, the Far East and Australasia.

His passion is simple: to demystify sport psychology and create practical, simple techniques to help soccer players win.

Table of Contents

1

Soccer is a Game of Mindset

Sit back and slide yourself into the boots of one of the world's greatest soccer[1] players. Become a legend for a few minutes. I'd like you to imagine a performance under the lights in the arena.

It's up to you who you choose. Maybe you're a Barcelona fan so you might picture a game through the eyes of Lionel Messi or Xavi Hernandes. You may like to mentally tuck yourself into the body of the enigmatic Italian striker Mario Balotelli or the dominant Manchester United forward Wayne Rooney. Perhaps you'd prefer to mirror the game of three time FIFA women's player of the year Birgit Prinz or take the form of a world class center back such as Rio Ferdinand who protects the penalty area as if his life depended on it. Or maybe visualizing yourself as a Brazilian playmaker such as Neymar or Marta Da Silva or the American great Mia Hamm is what excites you. If you're a goal keeper then you may look no further than the Spaniard Casillas, one of the world's best shot stoppers.

Now build a stadium in your mind. Wembley, the Azteca in Mexico, the Nou Camp or the Olympic Stadium in Rome. Somewhere where dreams are realized or broken. Somewhere big enough to dwarf the 22 players competing hard to win the prize. Put yourself on the pitch.

----

[1] In this book, I will interchangeably use the terms soccer and football, as well as soccer player and footballer.

Let's add your opponents. Make them good, seriously good. Quick, sharp, intelligent. That's who the world's best play against week in week out. That is their privilege and their burden. Now play....

Standing on the Shoulders of Giants

In your mind, play in the style of your chosen one. Compete hard, with passion, with commitment, with a will for victory that knows no limits. But as you picture this imaginary game - remember just how good your opponents are. Be realistic about the challenges they bring.

You try to find space, they cover it; you get on the ball, they press you hard leaving no time to make decisions. Who to pass to? Even with your head up you can only see opposition shirts; you press them, they throw a shape and ghost past you or play the simple pass that renders you irrelevant. You go to make a strong tackle, they ride your challenge, you cover but chase shadows. You launch yourself to win headers, they time their jumps better. You receive the ball but with little time to play it to a team mate.

You may have picked a world class footballer but you've got to play at your best. The opposition are mind benders. Their play can sap your energy, erase your confidence and distract your focus. The pitch is a whirlwind of information. Thousands of pieces of data are thrown at you at any one time. Your inner script reflects the complexity and speed of the game.

"Check left shoulder, watch the runners, stay tight, mark space, monitor ball and man, head up, track back, jump, challenge, find gaps, man on, show him inside... check shoulders... keep tight, keep tight."

And your brain doesn't help matters. It wants to dwell on the mistake you've made but that will just slow you down. It delights in sending your nervous system into overdrive as you go a goal down - ruining your coordination and technical execution. It craves an argument with the referee following a dubious decision that goes against you. It wants you to ball watch rather than letting you check the movements of the man you're marking. As you will discover throughout this book your brain is 'anti zone'. It is designed with inconsistency in mind, with a focus on problems rather than solutions. Not the kind of software you need to play your best every week.

A Game of Mindset

The design of your brain combined with the difficulty of the game means that soccer can beat you up, it really can! One match everything goes great. You drill passes into your team mates, you time every tackle perfectly, you are sharp and on your toes and seem to have the movement to find space to receive passes for the whole game. Controlling the ball is effortless. If you are a striker you get plenty of shots away and if you're a defender you always seem one step ahead of the opposition.

But another match might bring a different story. The game is a chore. Your legs feel heavy; your feet feel like they're sticking to the ground with glue. You are slow to react, you miss your passes and the opposition brush off your attempts to tackle them. On this day the striker can't get a shot on goal and the defender makes mistake after mistake allowing the opposition to nip in and bag a couple of goals.

Mindset: the origin of performance and the victim of performance.

To me, soccer is not just a physical challenge - it is a game of mindset. I say this with conviction but don't misunderstand me. Having a great mindset doesn't automatically invite you to tread the same turf as Pele, Maradona or George Best.

I'm not blind to the obvious fact that physicality, technical ability and tactical understanding are the main hallmarks of elite football. But having a mind strong enough to help you cope with the many challenges you face on and off the pitch can help you get the most from your football potential. And this is true whether you are a world class player in the Barcelona squad, whether you are striving to be a professional, whether you enjoy competing every weekend for your local team or whether you just enjoy a kick about with mates in an after work five-a-side league.

Step into my world

When you take a little time to think about your soccer brain, you step into my world. In my world how you talk to yourself on the pitch is just as important as your ability to trap and control the ball. In my world your body language is as vital a component of performance as the ability to head a crossed ball. In my world being thoroughly prepared for a match is more than just what you should eat and remembering to bring your boots to the big match.

My world is soccer psychology. And it is *your* soccer mindset that I want to help you with in this book.

Whenever I tell someone that I'm a soccer psychology consultant the response seems to vary from laughter to mild irritation. I guess the irritation comes from the presumption that multi-millionaire soccer players don't need their egos massaged or require techniques to help them focus. The money alone should be enough. My response to this is several fold.

Firstly being a professional athlete has never, and will never, protect someone from the challenges of life and the negative workings of the brain. Sports stars still have needs, wants, fears, values, experiences, worries, doubts, desires and hopes. They are human and they react and respond to adversity, to pressure situations and to the daily rigors of training like any other human would, with the same inconsistencies that make us who we are. Wealth isn't a cure for a lack of confidence on the ball. Nor does a thriving bank balance teach a gifted player how to deal with on pitch distractions or provide him with a manual for how to use the sports brain.

It must also be remembered that only 0.001% who start out on the journey to soccer stardom find their destination. The vast majority simply don't have the ability or the physical learning capability the very best have. But this doesn't mean they can't strive to be the best they can be. I work with clients, both professional and amateur, and as I say to all of them, I'm a soccer stretch *not* a soccer shrink. No matter what your innate physical gifts are - if you improve your mindset you can improve and stretch your soccer game.

Similarly, the laughter that meets my job title is no doubt down to a misconception about the game that plays out in front of people. The viewer sees a game that is quick, instinctive and simple. Why the need for psychology?

The Soccer Brain Works in Milliseconds

My sporting background is golf: a slow, methodical game in which mindset is accepted to play a large part in performance because there is so much time to think. Soccer is different and provides a stage where the scene changes every second. Whenever I sit at the bottom of a stand at ground level, or stand beside a pitch and watch a game in full flow I marvel at the speed of soccer. Players at the top of the world game today have approximately two seconds on the ball to make a decision before they are challenged. Every action they take, every motion they make must be executed at tremendous speed.

But when I watch soccer players competing I know there is something on the pitch working quicker than the game itself. Science has taught us that whilst football works in seconds the brain works in milliseconds. In fact we can be more accurate than that. Brain science has discovered that the brain makes sure people feel emotions 200 milliseconds after an event happens, and think consciously 500 milliseconds later.

It's mind blowing stuff. When a referee makes a decision a soccer player feels emotion as it's happening, and thinks about the decision instantly. And this is the same for any event on the pitch whether it's a goal conceded, a bad pass, or criticism from a team mate. Every event in the heat of battle brings with it an immediate emotional reaction and a set of thoughts designed to influence the player's next action.

As we will explore in this book, our response to events is not always what we want and not always the best for our soccer game. As this book unfolds you'll learn that a footballer has to be fantastic at dealing with his emotions and managing thought processes every single second of every single match. With feelings and thoughts rising to the surface in the blink of an eye - *soccer performance is tough to manage*. Technique, anticipation, awareness and decision making are affected, in the moment, by the functioning of the brain and by mindset.

And the murky waters of the soccer mindset become less clear when you examine the nature of the game.

The Inch that Makes the Difference

When I watch soccer I'm constantly in awe of the small differences that affect the result. A mistimed tackle, a poorly delivered pass, a weak shot, an over-hit cross, and a poorly timed run are a few of the things that factor together to win or lose games. An observant soccer fan will see this week in, week out, in parks and amateur soccer right the way through to games played in the English Premiership, La Liga, and Serie A.

There isn't a game that goes by where this isn't the case. Allow me to illustrate

Chapter 1

this by using two examples. The first takes us back to 1996 and the semi-finals of the European Championships. England, the hosts of the tournament, was playing Germany. At one-all in extra time the game was tight. This was a tournament when FIFA, the governing body of world soccer, decided to play a format called Golden Goal in extra time, meaning that the first team to score instantly won the tie.

Deep into extra time England had a glorious opportunity to score. The enigmatic and enormously talented English player Paul Gascoigne agonizingly found himself an inch away from latching onto a ball played across the front of the goal. Gascoigne had run from deep into a great position inside the German penalty area and, as he noticed his team mate lining up to drill the ball across the penalty area, he took a couple of strides closer to the goal. The 80,000 English supporters held their breath as they saw what Gascoigne saw, the opportunity to become a national hero. But Gascoigne hesitated for a split second, and whilst he stretched his leg as far as he could - he missed contact by an inch. 30 minutes later England was out of the competition losing in a nail biting penalty shootout.

Fast forward to 21st May 2008 and the Champions League Final between Manchester United and Chelsea in the Luzhniki Stadium in Russia. The Champions League is one of the world's greatest cup competitions played out by Europe's leading club teams. Always full of drama - 2008 didn't disappoint.

The game between the two English clubs had ebbed and flowed and after goals from Cristiano Ronaldo and Frank Lampard, it had gone to that most agonizing of match deciders, penalty kicks. Ronaldo turned villain when he missed his penalty and Chelsea, vying for their first European trophy since the 1990s only needed their captain John Terry to slot home from twelve yards to win the Champions League. But twelve yards can seem like twenty under pressure and after a hesitant run up John Terry slipped as he struck the ball which collided with the right hand post and agonizingly for Terry stayed out of the goal. An inch or so to the left and the trophy was won. Instead the shootout continued and following another missed penalty Chelsea would lose, beaten in the most painful of circumstances to their English rivals.

These stories provide just a couple of examples of a worldwide soccer phenomenon. In every game, every single day, the world over, from World Cup matches to college games to fun five-a-side matches - *soccer is a game of inches*. Matches are won and lost on the odd misplaced pass and mistimed tackle. If you were to take a few minutes to think about your game, the game of the players you coach, or the games played by your favorite team - how often have performances and results hinged on these inches? A loss may have been down to a defender losing a little focus against a quick witted striker who managed to get in front of him and score the only goal of the game. A win may have been a result of your team mate playing with confidence and jumping an inch higher than the center back to glance a header into the corner of the net.

Soccer is a game of inches and therefore it is vital that every player is equipped with simple soccer psychology techniques to deal with the tough breaks, the dodgy decisions, the close shaves, the near misses and human mistakes that the game constantly delivers.

The Multiplier Effect

So an inch here, an inch there, mediates the performance and the result of the games you play. Working on your soccer psychology can influence whether those inches fall *for* you or *against* you. Another compelling reason to work on your mindset lies in a concept that I find influences the journey of every soccer player. It's what I call the multiplier effect.

Imagine this: your coach notices that you tend to switch off at crucial moments during the game. He gives you a couple of ideas to maintain focus and manage the distractions that come your way as the game develops. These ideas work nicely for you. You feel slightly more in control of your focus, perhaps a little sharper with your concentration.

This new feeling of focus enables you to trap a ball a little better. It's slightly more under your control which helps you to get your passes away a bit quicker. Knowing that you can distribute the ball before your opponent challenges you gives you an injection of confidence. With a bit more belief surging through your body you have a period of stand-out performances which win the praise of your coaches and your team mates. More confidence! More belief!

You now find it easier to get your head up and look around you. With greater awareness you can see the movement of the opposition more clearly and the runs your team mates make. Such vision allows you to play some devastating balls through to your team mates and you are quicker to track and close down the opposition when they have the ball. More praise! More confidence! More belief! Better consistency of performance. And all this started from a small seed planted when a coach gave you a few tips to improve your focus.

I have simplified the process greatly and often it operates at a level that is close to intangible and almost impossible to define, but it's very real. It's something I see week-to-week with my clients.

Just as the leg bone is connected to the knee bone and the knee bone is connected to the thigh bone, so the brain is connected to the body and thus the mental, technical, tactical and physical sides of the game of soccer are inextricably linked. They work in harmony and an improvement in one area has a knock on effect on the other areas. Of course this works both ways. A loss of confidence can diminish both technical and tactical execution. As the great Spanish manager Rafa Benitez points out: *"What is physical work without desire, technical skill without concentration, tactical skill without confidence?"*

The multiplier effect is one for the obsessive soccer player or coach to study; the ones who don't just have the will to win, but who also have the will to prepare to win.

Wanting to win is the easy part. Whether you play a five-a-side every Monday, whether you are a ten-year-old playing for your school team, or whether you are playing for Brazil in the World Cup final the likelihood is that everyone who is playing against you wants to win as well. But the reality is it's the person and team who are the most prepared - who gives himself or themselves the best opportunity to win – who normally prevails.

And this gets to the heart of soccer psychology. Working on your mindset gives you that edge over your opponents. Having simple techniques to play with unshakeable belief and correct focus as well as being able to bounce back with confidence from a defeat will have more influence over the result of your next match than the person or team who ignore mindset techniques, prepare less, but who have an extreme desire to win.

You Can Do This without Sweating

So a small shift in soccer mindset can lead to a big change in performance. This is my mantra, my philosophy, my passion. I know that if I can help a soccer player sharpen his thinking on and off the pitch by as little as a few percent his team mates and coaches will see enormous improvement in the quality and consistency of his play.

Many soccer players and coaches rebel against psychology, mostly because they don't want to explore the unknown or the complicated. My passion is to demystify performance psychology for them. I love creating very simple ideas, delivered in the language of soccer, that they can take away and use on the training pitch and on match day.

This doesn't mean that what I preach and teach is always easy to apply. There is a difference between simple and easy. It takes time, effort, and practice for a player to improve his soccer psychology. One cannot 'master' the mental game. It's not like riding a bicycle. The mental side of soccer comes in waves and fits and starts. It's an everyday thing! Just as you have to regularly fill a car with fuel to keep it going so an athlete has to fill his mind with thoughts that aid the likelihood of a confident, positive performance.

If you were to ask me what I love about my job I could come up with a lot of answers. I do love my job! But if I was to pinpoint one thing it would be the fact that I can positively influence performance by discussing techniques in the comfort of a chair and with a cup of coffee in hand. This isn't because I'm physically lazy but because I love the idea that a player can improve a physical sport without breaking sweat. Language is the main tool for learning and I love to see a soccer player improve his game on the pitch as a result of simply discussing the challenges he has, and imagining what the game would be like if those challenges magically disappeared.

In this book

This book will challenge the way you approach football, whether it's how you play or how you view the game. And the following pages will be demanding of you. You will be required to look at soccer as more than just a series of actions. The mental mechanics underlying the skill, the technical execution and tactical discipline you witness as you watch soccer will be examined.

You'll learn that in soccer the soft skills are the hard skills. A player's confidence can disappear as quickly and as quietly as it arrived. That all important capacity to focus may be enjoyed in fleeting moments but often distracted by the nature of the game and by the complexity of the brain. In a sport of emotion you will read how the careers of players with huge talent slow as a result of the burden of expectation, the difficulty of self-management and because of the grip negative feelings can have over clarity of thought as the pressure of performance builds. Most importantly you will be offered solutions to the mental challenges the beautiful game presents.

Chapter 1

Whatever mindset challenges you face in soccer, whether it's the confidence to play, dealing with distraction or managing destructive emotions this book will provide you with a solution and a set of tangible techniques that can be tested on and off the pitch. And the best news of all is that building a new set of thoughts and shifting a few playing philosophies can seriously improve your soccer game.

A different soccer world

I hope this book takes you into a different soccer world, a world often hidden from view. Over the course of the book, I will introduce you not only to the soccer brain but also to some of the colorful characters who strive every day to use their mind to improve their soccer performance. Some of these players are just starting out in their careers, readying themselves for the rocky road that is progression. Others are seasoned professionals and household names who have known the highs and joys of promotion but also the lows and heartache of relegation.

Be proactive as you read. Exercise your memory, your imagination, your thinking and explore your capacity to experience the feelings the greatest soccer players on the planet enjoy. Included in the text are some of the Tweets I post everyday on the Twitter website that aim to get soccer players, coaches and fans debating the performance mindset. I hope they are thought provoking.

The book is not my CV. Some chapters involve case studies from my playbook, while others tell the tale of soccer players who have figured it out for themselves, or who have sought help from sport psychologists whose voices are similar to mine. Clients, friends, or merely interviewees - they all have a story to tell and I relate their tale to the functioning of the brain, to the nuances of mindset, and to simple psychology techniques that will improve your soccer game.

The soccer players in this book come from different backgrounds, have differing personalities, and have experienced various degrees of success. But they also have several things in common. They all love the game, they are all hungry to win and improve, and they all have something to teach you about your soccer mindset.

2

How Elvis Found Graceland

Are you a golf fan? If so, take a few moments to think about the powerful swing of Tiger Woods that enables him to crunch the ball down the fairway. Perhaps you prefer basketball? Close your eyes and picture the spring of Michael Jordan as he floats through a cluster of opposing players to claim another dunk. Enjoy the Olympics? Envisage Michael Phelps, the greatest swimmer ever, gliding through the water with finesse but with such speed he appears to finish the pool's length just as his initial dive into the water completes its momentum.

When I think about sports competitors with enormous self-belief my mind is immediately drawn to a vast array of champions. I hear the boxing braggadocio Muhammad Ali whose outrageous public declarations of genius not only enhanced his own belief but unnerved and lowered the certainty of his opposition. I marvel at the quality of Beckham and Ronaldo free kicks, bending shots that can only be executed with exacting technique. I visualize the dynamic movement of Roger Federer twisting, turning, and stretching to win every point, every game and every set. I think about the power of the Williams sisters, the accuracy of golfer Annika Sorenstam, and the unparalleled speed of Usain Bolt.

When you watch these champions all you see is their body: the technical precision, the tactical acumen and the physical strength and effort. My obsession is with their mind – the mindset that allows their body to execute day in day out. The mindset that enables their body to deliver under the most intense pressure and helps their body to improve after every training session.

I take this obsession out on the road with me – to soccer clubs, organizations and to individual sessions with some of the best footballers playing today. I also enjoy spreading my obsession out into the football community by using social media. Throughout this book I want to introduce you to the sound bites my Twitter followers read every day (twitter id: *Danabrahams77*) These short take home messages will neatly sum up key points from each chapter and help you digest the psychology of soccer in less than 140 characters. Let's start with this one:

It is a soccer player's ability to manage his mindset that separates him from his peers

Of all the mindset qualities one can think of - it is self-belief and confidence that tend to be the most talked about, the most sought after, and the most elusive.

Self-belief

It doesn't take ownership of a psychologist's couch to know that the possession of self-belief is a sportsman's *must have* acquisition. Its presence is where excellence begins. Yet few footballers know or understand how to build and maintain self-belief. Some deem it impossible to control, while others have never thought of exercising its management. Similarly most allow it to come and go like their weekly fixture list. This abandonment is not an indication that they care little about self-belief, more that they just don't know how to develop it.

All too often a soccer coach will point to the training pitch as the path to self-belief. Many coaches preach the simple equation 'building skill leads to belief' but as we will explore in this chapter - that simplistic viewpoint is incomplete and less powerful a cocktail than adding mindset into the mix.

Self-belief and Confidence

Self-belief and confidence are closely related. To me, self-belief in sport refers to the bigger picture: how you feel about yourself as a competitor. In contrast confidence in sport is how you feel about achieving success in a given moment - such as in training or in a match, or while executing a skill such as heading or tackling.

Self-belief fuels confidence. It is impossible to be confident on match day if you have no self-belief. It is possible to be confident on match day some of the time if you have some self-belief. But if you ooze self-belief, if self-belief is flowing around your body and through every pore, then you have a great chance of playing with consistent confidence. And high self-belief delivers bulletproof confidence. Have a bad game and high self-belief means you won't be as susceptible to a slump in form.

Self-belief is to confidence what foundations are to a house or an engine is to a car. My job is to give soccer players ideas and techniques to build a strong foundation, or if we're using the car comparison, then a *top class engine*. In fact, I'm trying to pimp their engine and soup up their car by increasing its power!

Self-belief to confidence is what an engine is to a car. A footballer without techniques to improve his self-belief won't move forward

Self-belief and Me

I myself know a lot about self-belief or at least a lack of it. I know that as a small time professional golfer who ground around the satellite tours in Europe I struggled to manage the belief I had in *myself* as a golfer.

I would stand on the first tee and look at my competitors who all appeared very tall and very strong and very skillful. They all had better swings than me and their putting strokes flowed back and through in a perfect pendulum-like motion. Of course this wasn't true. I had a very good swing and a very solid putting stroke and no one I knew on the golf circuit had Superman powers. But I didn't believe

13

this because I saw myself as inferior to other golf professionals. And it was this self-image that dictated the belief I had in myself as a golfer - *just as your self-image strongly influences the belief you have in you*. It is self-image that I want to focus on in this chapter and in so doing we will start with the story of Elvis.

Calling Elvis

Elvis stared out onto the training pitch with the intensity of someone who needed something to work. Anything!

A few of the young apprentices were still practicing out on the pitch ahead of him but he didn't see them. His bright blue eyes looked forward but his mind focused inwardly. A small smile enveloped his face as he searched his memory banks. He'd hit upon something. He turned to speak.

"Stay with the image," I said. I didn't want him to lose the new catalogue of pictures he'd obviously envisioned, so he moved his head back and returned to his fragile memory. Very slowly he closed his eyes and immersed himself in his private cinema once more. I prompted him further.

"You can tell me the details in a few minutes. Just take some quiet time to picture the game. Use as many of your senses as you can. What were you doing? What did you see? What did you feel? What did you hear?"

I wanted Elvis to have a rich sensory experience. Elvis was shifting his self-image. He was re-building his self-belief. He was finding his Graceland.

When David Rouse, Queens Park Rangers' goalkeeping coach said that he wanted me to work with Elvis my first thoughts were 'funky haircut, 50s music, Blue Suede Shoes'; I didn't think 'Latvian, shaven head, goalkeeper.' But this was what confronted me after David explained himself. "*This kid is good. Technically he can play and physically he's sharp, but he needs help. He's lost a lot of belief, partly through being injured but also through not playing much*". He continued: "*He's probably going to be released at the end of the season but I'm passionate about helping this kid stay in the pro game. He's good enough.*" And that was how I got to meet a young Latvian goalkeeper called Elvis Putnins.

When Elvis came to England he spoke little or no English. The son of a lorry driver he had done what many young Eastern European soccer players have to do to reach for the soccer stars - he had to leave his homeland and seek his fortune in one of the major leagues in Europe.

Some initial success as a youth team player and some caps at international Under-21 level helped him win a contract at Queens Park Rangers (QPR) in England, which, at the time of his arrival, was a medium sized Championship club (the second tier in English soccer). The club would soon find success and promotion to the English Premier League but Elvis's own progress didn't mirror that of Rangers. He stalled!

Lost Belief

Being from Latvia it made sense to Elvis to work as hard as he could on his technique. Goalkeeping is a very technical profession and given the analytical nature and cool temperament of Eastern Europeans it has now become fashionable for football scouts from Europe's top clubs to explore Eastern Bloc countries for shot stopping talent.

Elvis reasonably assumed that his self-belief would grow as his technical ability and tactical understanding of the game improved. He had, after all, always been a confident goalkeeper never needing to spend time managing his thinking and his temperament. He didn't even know how to. But Elvis was training at a club which competed at a level much higher than his previous teams. He had very few opportunities to play and when he did - he played poorly, at a standard that David Rouse assured me was well below that which he displayed during training. Elvis was able to do it, but not with enough consistency and certainly not in the heat of battle.

In our first session together Elvis told me that he had lost the belief he always had in himself. He didn't see himself as capable of being a professional goal keeper anymore. At night he would think about making mistakes and when he woke up he would reinforce failure by rehearsing those mistakes in his mind again. He looked around the training ground and saw better players than him. To him the other goalkeepers who trained at QPR were unbeatable, while he felt he was slow, sluggish and scared. Injury hadn't helped and by the 30 minute mark of our first session it was obvious that the goalkeeper who had once seen himself as destined for the stars was fragile, mentally lost with a shattered self-belief. The image he had of himself had changed. My job was to reverse this mental trend.

You in the Mirror

Do you recognize Elvis's challenge? Perhaps the stage isn't football but some other area of your life? Maybe you've had a promotion at work that involves responsibilities and skills that you've never seen yourself as good at (e.g. presenting or holding meetings with colleagues)? In your new role you struggle to see yourself capturing the attention of your audience. Subsequently your first presentation is disastrous.

If you're a little younger and still at school possibly your ability to learn mathematics has slowed because you can't *see* yourself understanding the complicated equations that you have to learn. As a result you fear the lessons and hope you won't be asked to answer a question in front of everyone else and be made to look foolish.

Our lives are heavily influenced by the images we have of ourselves in our mind. We all have lots of self-images. We have a specific image for being a husband or wife, a son or daughter. These images may be different to the image we have of ourselves in our job which in turn may vary from the images we hold of ourselves as a friend.

The person who has a strong image of himself as a husband may have a weaker image of himself as a public speaker. The different images help and hinder us as we make our way through life. There are many variations and no hard and fast rules. Self-image can be quite chaotic. Feel free to take a little time to think about all of your self-images. It's an interesting exercise to do.

Of course if you play soccer you have an image of you as a soccer player. This is your soccer image. Your soccer image refers to the pictures and movies you have in your mind related to your soccer.

Every soccer player has a soccer image - an image housed in their mind related to how they see themselves as players

When you think about your soccer game what do you see? Take a few minutes to allow your mind to build a small picture book or short movie reel. What images does your mind settle on? Do you see crisp, sharp movement or lethargic, slow actions? Does your brain direct you toward confident completed passes or anxious wayward balls?

When you think of your team mates does your mind deliver a confident message to your body, one that says "*I'm the best choice for the team*" accompanied by a vision of you leading your team mates and being the stand out player? What is the content of your mind's trailer when it comes to the opposition or players competing at a higher level to you?

Is your mental movie one of *possibility*, *progress* and *achievement* or does your inner screen just display other footballers as bigger, better and stronger?

This is a simple but important exercise to do every few weeks because it gives you an idea of your soccer image. Be honest with yourself. Don't try to manipulate the images in your mind just yet. Allow them to flow naturally so you have a good indication of where you are now with your soccer image.

It is important to understand that you don't just have one soccer image. You have lots!

If you're a striker you will have images relating to your ability to move, to score, to hold the ball up, to find space, to win headers, to hit the target, to play under pressure and to focus. As a goalkeeper your inner movies will relate to your ability to make reaction saves, to come for a crossing ball, to get in the right position on a one-versus-one, to save a penalty, to command your box and the back line, and to perform confidently under pressure.

Every position demands a different set of skills and offers a different set of challenges, and how much you believe in yourself when it comes to those skills and challenges is influenced by the images you have of them.

Two contrasting self-images

Phil and Lee were strikers who played for a professional youth team I consulted with several years ago. Both had ability and were of equal physicality but Phil was scoring and Lee wasn't. In separate sessions I asked them what they saw in their mind when they thought about themselves as a striker. Their answers were completely different.

Phil: "*I see goals. I love to run behind the defense, use my pace. Get an inch and bang, a goal. Hold the ball up, great... lay it off, get it back then boom, take a shot. I see space. That's what the best see, and man that's what I see too. Space means goals in my book, I don't have to think where that target is, it's there I know it is. It's just about finding that space.*"

Lee: "*My job is to score but it's tough to. As a striker you play with your back to goal. I can score but I see a lot of misses when I think about my job. I work hard for the team, that's what I'm there for as well. My movement is important. Move well and I give myself chances to score. I must remember that. I see the penalty area. It's always crowded which makes it tough to find gaps. Sometimes you do. I can see myself finding gaps, but not all the time. Sometimes the defense fills it so well.*"

Which one of these players has an exciting image, an exciting picture? Which one of these players is going to feel like he can score? Which one of these players would you pick for your team?

A footballer will never perform better than the image he has of himself

Ruling your Game

Your soccer image rules your soccer game because these inner pictures and movies influence:

- how much belief you have in yourself to learn and improve
- how good you feel you can be
- how confident you are for match day

A high level of belief leading to match day confidence is so often accompanied by focus, determination, effort, commitment, freedom and discipline. And it all stems from your soccer image.

I know how important your soccer image is because I see the outcomes in action every day. I watch young players who have great skill and great potential underachieve because they don't *see* themselves as first team players. They are unable to *see* themselves competing with the very best, even though they are more than capable of eventually doing so.

I have had conversations with leading coaches who display enormous frustration because some of their players fail to execute training ground tactics in matches. Why? Quite often because they don't *see* themselves as able to compete with the opposition. And I have had numerous sessions with players who are suffering from a slump in form because they can only *see* their bad games, their weaknesses and their mistakes.

You Create You

I don't believe that you are born with your soccer images. I believe you develop them yourself. To my mind you build them in 3 ways:

- by your perception
- by your memory
- by your imagination

These 3 ways of thinking influence how you *see* yourself as a footballer. Let's take a little time to look at how negative soccer images are developed.

Perhaps you are a striker and you've just had a bad game. You're very disappointed and you keep replaying in your mind the bad moments, especially the chances you've missed. You see in your mind's eye the shot you miskicked and the easy header you glanced straight at the keeper. You replay these snapshots over and over on the way home from the match, over breakfast the next day and into training three days later.

This is your *memory* feeding your soccer image and this constant rehearsal of what went wrong influences how you perceive the game. It's not helped that your team mate texted you to tell you he couldn't believe you missed that gilt-edged chance to score. It makes you assume that others think you're no good as a striker. And you reinforce this by thinking you're no good up front. This is your *perception*: you perceive you are no good as a striker. Next, your perception is going to feed into your all-powerful *imagination*.

You will now spend time imagining all the missed shots you're going to have in the next game. Imagination then loops back to your thinking. You think about being dropped and you imagine your replacement scoring goals and preventing you from ever getting back in the team.

Then up pops your memory again as you picture the chances you missed in the last game and you curse your poor performance. Memory, perception and imagination - bullying your positive soccer image, and turning it into a series of destructive clips. This really is football psychology in action. This player is developing a negative striker image.

Is he going to be confident on match day if he keeps feeding these negative images to himself? Is he going to be on his toes, alert and alive, ready to take an opportunity to score when it comes his way? Is he going to make effective decisions under pressure or have the kind of killer movement that unlocks the tightest of defenses? If he is rehearsing these images day in day out - is he going to train effectively? Are his coaches going to see a confident, focused striker?

This striker needs to understand that what he rehearses in his mind becomes his soccer image. And this image influences his self-belief. And in turn his self-belief dictates his confidence to perform under pressure on match day. Your soccer image is like a bank account. The more money you put into a bank account the more interest you get. The more positive your thoughts the better your soccer image, the more confident you will be, and the better you will play. Spend more than you make, and your bank account goes into the red where you will be charged by the bank. Think more negative thoughts than positive thoughts and you will have a poor soccer image; you will lose confidence and play worse.

*It is your memory, perception and imagination
that drives your soccer image and subsequently
your self-belief*

Tiger's Tale

To me Tiger Woods is an example of someone who had an extraordinarily strong self-image for his sport and it took some extraordinary life events to change and damage his self-image.

Tiger is, to me, an example of a walking psychological phenomenon. The training he received from his father growing up was awe inspiring. At the age of 6 Tiger fell asleep to the sound of positive subliminal messages. He heard a voice from under his pillow, where his father (Earl Woods) placed a tape every night with messages such as "You will move mountains" and "You will be the best". Did this make a huge difference to his career? Who knows! But it set him on his journey that for over a decade helped him become one of the most mentally tough sportsmen ever to grace the planet.

"Every time I play, in my own mind, I am the favorite." - Tiger Woods

At the age of twelve Tiger started to have regular visits to a clinical sports psychologist called Dr. Jay Brunza who helped him hone his visualization and imagination. And finally throughout his teenage years Tiger was exposed to a concentration technique that helped build his phenomenal focus.

Earl Woods played with Tiger virtually every day, and from the age of 13 Earl would regularly do small things that might put Tiger off. He would cough when he got to the top of his backswing or rattle his clubs when Tiger drew his putter back. As Earl Woods recounted later, before his death, it would frustrate Tiger immensely but he knew it was an important exercise to help hone his focus ability before he entered the tough world of professional golf.

"I did envisage being this successful as a player." - Tiger Woods

And so Tiger listened and learned and grew a strong golf image, perhaps stronger than there's ever been in professional golf. He saw himself competing with and beating the best and when he got to the course I would take an educated guess that his mindset was *"I'm Tiger, I'm here and I'm going to win. Be afraid, be very afraid"*. And win he did, until the events of December 2009 unfolded.

Tiger as a golfer is a hero of mine and I certainly don't want to professionally criticize him. But at the time of writing this book Tiger is not the same golfer who used to grace the fairways with such confidence and assuredness, almost arrogance. People can quibble that his current demise is down to his poor physical shape or the swing changes he's currently making. Both ring true. But for me the accusations and subsequent acceptance of marital misdemeanors has changed Tiger's golf image and subsequently has damaged his performances on the course. Just as importantly, the incidents have changed the image other professional golfers have of him. They no longer see him as the flawless golfing machine who conducts himself perfectly on and off the course. They now believe they can compete with him in the biggest tournaments.

Tiger Woods's challenge at the moment is an example of what can happen when you don't nourish your own mind with positive, confident images. It must be enormously difficult to do that when you have had the kind of life upheavals that Tiger has had over the past few years. I'm sure Tiger will keep working every day technically, physically and mentally to come back a stronger golfer. I'm sure he's up for that challenge.

Using Elvis's Memory Banks

Let's be clear, sometimes my job is easy. Sometimes it's so obvious what a player needs to do with his mindset. This was the case with Elvis. He was continuously remembering and rehearsing his bad games and his mistakes and errors. He was feeding his soccer image with internal soccer movies that prevented him from developing any feelings of self-belief. So we got to work and basically this is what we did.

Me: *Elvis, take a few minutes to think about your very best game over the past couple of seasons.*

Elvis: *Okay that would be an under 21 game for Latvia against Romania. I was awesome! (he said this with a big grin on his face... bingo!)*

Me: *Tell me more about it....*

And so Elvis told me more about that game. In fact we spoke about that game for half an hour. We went into small details. What he was wearing, how he prepared, what he did in the changing room before kick-off, how he felt in the first ten minutes of the match, what his body language was like, and what he was saying to himself and others during the game. I wanted to know everything.

"Walking out I knew. You just know don't you, that you're going to play well. I felt strong and calm. A little nervous but calm inside. Boy I was ready to make

some great saves. Warm up was great. I was sharp, ready. The ball looked big. The first 10 minutes really set the tone of the game for me. Got my finger tips to a great shot and came and caught a tough hanging ball. The strikers got nowhere near my leap."

And as we spoke I could see Elvis start to mentally pick up. He was animated as we discussed the game. He smiled. His voice became louder and more intonated. He had a measurable physical response that paralleled how he now felt inside: warm and happy with a feeling of belief. His soccer image was changing.

*Positive pictures every day lead to
big hits of belief*

Now try this yourself. Try nourishing your soccer image. Start to remember your very best game from the past couple of seasons. Play your best game movie in your mind. See and feel the movement you had, the shots you took, and the tackles you made. What were you like in the air? Were you strong and committed? Were you a leader: loud, dominant and demanding? See and feel in your mind as many of the positive actions you executed. Were you first to the ball? Were you constantly switched on, talking to yourself, energized, alert and athletic?

Were you solid at the back or were you a box-to-box midfielder who commanded the middle of the pitch by playing penetrating through balls and by tracking runners? Were you a goal keeper who played with the confidence to climb above the opposition in the penalty box and collect the crossing ball with ease? See and feel the runs you made and the body shape that allowed you to view the runs of your team mates and the opposition.

I'd like you to do this exercise every day. I'd like you to feed your mind with the plays from your best game. As you do so - allow a wave of belief to flow through your body. Enjoy the process. Make your mind movie big and bold and bright with surround sound. Use as many senses as possible especially what you saw, what you felt and what you heard. In the next chapter I will talk a little more about the art and science of picturing your football.

I think constantly about my strengths. I dwell on best moments. I resonate my best games. I know my weaknesses & love 2 try 2 improve them

Your Time Travel Machine

Are you committed to the process of building a powerful, bulletproof soccer image? Are you excited about feeding your mind with images, pictures and movies of you playing at your very best? Are you now beginning to realize that you can take complete control of your soccer image, self-belief and match day confidence? If I've captured your imagination let's take things a step further. I want you to keep a journal or, as I like to call it, a 'Soccer Bible'.

In this journal I want you to write down your 3 best ever games. Write them in detail just as we've discussed before. This will give you something to come back to every day that can help build and maintain a strong soccer image. It will help you take control of the memories you have of your football.

When writing down your 3 best games remember key moments such as the runs you made, the tackles, blocks, passes and headers you won. Add feelings to your story – "I felt strong, confident and powerful" and "I felt like I was unbeatable" – these are exciting images to remember and to reinforce. If your friends or loved ones were watching you what do you think they would have seen? Write their viewpoint down as well.

Allow me to give you a good example of an entry you can make into your Soccer Bible. This is a segment from the Soccer Bible of a young central defender who plays amateur football.

"It was a game against our local rivals. I was nervous but I felt like I could play well that day. I warmed up well. If I was on the sidelines watching myself I'd have seen great body language, looking really dominant. I would have heard my voice encouraging others. I would have seen myself show the ball in the small sided warm game. I felt alive, active and full of energy. I remember saying to myself "Come on I can do this today, I'm going to have a great one". I really felt in charge of myself. Just before kick-off I was loud in the changing room,

encouraging everyone, shaking hands, high fiving. I felt really upbeat at that moment. I wasn't captain but felt I was louder than him anyway.

Although I didn't see much of the ball in the opening 10 minutes I kept myself busy. I pinned the striker on a few corners, made sure he didn't get near the ball. That gave me confidence, knowing I could out muscle him.

When we went a goal down I still remember feeling calm. I was pleased I encouraged our goalkeeper as he'd just made a mistake for the goal. I was winning all my headers and I read the game well. I felt committed in every tackle. I felt strong, strong, strong.

I love the way my head was up all the time. Not only for confidence but also for awareness. I had time to think. I could see the opportunities and the dangers."

This entry into his Soccer Bible helps this young defender remember what he does when he does it well. It highlights key terms such as "strong" and "out muscle" and "head up for awareness". I love the fact it's vivid and recalls the great game from his own eyes as well as the eyes of the crowd. It's emotional. It feels exciting and special. This is what I want for your Soccer Bible.

This process will help you remember you at your best more easily. The words you write will spark your memory and evoke the inner pictures you have stored. It's like turning on a light in a darkened room. Flick the switch and you can see the room rather than fumbling in the dark. Log the details of your best games in your Soccer Bible and you can switch on exciting, positive and confident pictures every time you read or glance at it.

Commit to reading your best games at least once a day. Elvis chooses to put a narrative of his best games on his fridge and by his bed. He knows that when he wants a glass of juice he has an opportunity to train his mindset. He knows that as his eyes glance at the paper magnetized to the front of the fridge he will see the words "Latvia versus Romania, Under 21 match" and as he quenches his thirst he gets to saturate his soccer image with positive pictures. He also knows that when he wakes every morning he will glimpse the same words that sit by his bed. A small injection of belief is just the tonic for this young goalkeeper first thing in the morning.

By training his memory, will Elvis be the next Peter Schmeichel? Maybe, maybe not. But what Elvis does know is that as he turns 20, a very young age for a goalkeeper, and as he leaves QPR for another club, just as he is able to develop his technical skill he is now able to work on his mindset. As he continues to shape and use his memory he takes a step closer to a strong soccer image. And I believe Elvis will do well because he has more to his armory than just his memory. He also uses his imagination. He has learnt that it is not only important to remember his very best games, but that he must use this blueprint to rehearse future success. The next chapter will further explore another technique Elvis is using to find his Graceland.

3

Daydreaming

I think all footballers do it.

Certainly my clients do it - without me telling them they should do it. They do it without their coaches telling them it helps. They perhaps do it even when they don't think they do. Former England goalkeeper David James does it a lot: *"I do it in the hotel room before the game, do it on the bus and do it on the pitch..."* Fernando Torres does it and so does Didier Drogba. Their athletic cousins do it on the court, the course, and the track.

I'm talking about picturing performance. I'm referring to that quiet time when a sports competitor immerses himself in a bubble of focus and builds a mental map of the game he wants to play. In this chapter I will challenge you to use your imagination. We will discuss how your daydreams feed your soccer image and how you can manage them so they become a mental blueprint for your game.

The Awakening of Sport Psychology

The 1980s brought infamy, drama and compelling action to the football pitch. In 1981 Ricky Villa, one of the first foreign players to play in the top flight of English football, went on a mazy run in the FA Cup final for Spurs against Manchester City. He split open their defense and scored a goal that many regard as one of the best the world's greatest domestic cup competition has ever seen.

Chapter 3

In 1982 soccer fans witnessed the emotional 'Tardelli cry' named after the emphatic celebration that followed the goal that won the World Cup for Italy. Italy triumphed despite the incredible collection of players that Brazil fielded that year. They had Socrates, Zico, Falcao and Eder, probably the greatest international team never to have won the World Cup.

1986 brought controversy when the world's leading player Diego Maradona, infamously declared that his handballed World Cup quarter final goal against England was scored by the 'Hand of God'. And what football fan could forget Marco Van Basten's wonder goal in the European Championship final in 1988: the immaculately struck volley from the edge of the area that somehow managed to dip over the outstretched arms of the Russian goalkeeper. No shortage of drama during the 1980s; a decade of incidents that lit up the beautiful game on a global scale.

At the same time many American universities were becoming interested in the influence the brain and mind had on sports performance. Elite sport was becoming more and more competitive and world class competitors in all sports demanded new ways to improve and beat the opposition.

Towards the end of the decade sport psychologist William Straub, working at one of those colleges, demonstrated the extraordinary power of the mind. In a revolutionary test he asked students to throw 50 darts at a board and then embark on a special training program. After initial scores were counted he split the students up into different groups. Some were told not to play darts again until they came back for another test eight weeks later. Another group practiced throwing darts for 30 minutes, five days a week, for eight weeks. A third group alternated between physical practice and picturing themselves throwing darts. They were told to see themselves positioned at the throwing line, to feel the dart in their fingers, to feel it release, to see and hear the dart hitting the bull's eye, and to allow themselves to experience the satisfaction they would feel at throwing accurate darts.

After eight weeks, the group who hadn't practiced physically or mentally showed no improvements. The group that practiced daily improved by an average of 67 points. But the group that used both practice combined with 'picturing throwing' improved by up to 165 points: an incredible improvement and a remarkable difference between the mentally trained group and the group who just trained physically.

By asking people to use their imagination in a constructive way Straub demonstrated that sports skills can be developed more quickly and executed better when training covers both body and mind. His scientific findings, alongside outcomes from other similar research studies, prompted coaches from all sports to start telling the sports world about the benefits of training mindset and mentality. This made sense to those who wanted to be the best in their given sport.

Olympians, golfers and tennis players started seeing psychologists to get the *head edge*. Coaches went on mental training programs to increase their knowledge of how the brain works in pressure situations. Soon individuals in team sports started to develop their minds. If they wanted to be in the starting line-up they needed an edge over the other players in their squad. Soccer players needed to find ways to sharpen their mind to defend better, pass more confidently, tackle with greater intensity, and score more goals.

A soccer player should exercise his mind every day just as he does his muscles

Wayne Rooney

The young Wayne Rooney scored goals. A lot of them! He scored 114 in 29 games for the Everton Under-10 team. From a young age he knew where the net was. He made his first team debut at just 16 years old but it wasn't until 5 days before his 17th birthday that the soccer world stood up and took notice.

In October 2002 Arsenal FC was *the team* to beat in the English Premier League. They hadn't lost in 30 games and Arsene Wenger's side was probably confident of making that 31 games when they travelled to Goodison Park, the home of Everton FC, on October 19th. Wayne Rooney had other ideas.

With the game destined for a draw, Rooney took the ball down 15 yards outside the penalty area. He started to run with the ball at a nervous Arsenal defense, and seeing them back away he tried his luck from 30 yards out. He struck the ball powerfully, bending it past the outstretched leg of Arsenal defender Sol Campbell and past the desperate dive of goalkeeper David Seaman. The ball struck the bottom of crossbar and dived into the net. With that 30 yard strike arrived a new

Chapter 3

footballing hero.

The audacious goal was scored through ability, technique, and vision, but also through mindset. Rooney has spoken a little about how, since being a very young player, he has visualized game patterns and goal scoring situations to enhance his performance.

"Part of my preparation is I go and ask the kit man what color we're wearing – if it's red top, white shorts, white socks or black socks. Then I lie in bed the night before the game and visualize myself scoring goals or doing well. You're trying to put yourself in that moment and trying to prepare yourself, to have a 'memory' before the game. I don't know if you'd call it visualizing or dreaming, but I've always done it, my whole life. When I was younger, I used to visualize myself scoring wonder goals, stuff like that. From 30 yards out, dribbling through teams. You used to visualize yourself doing all that, and when you're playing professionally, you realize it's important for your preparation." (Source: The Guardian 17/5/12)

What was Rooney doing the night before that career defining moment? I can take an educated guess. I believe that Rooney was sitting on his sofa or lying on his bed picturing how he wanted to play. I believe he was immersed in his own private cinema rehearsing how he wanted to compete against Arsenal. I believe his inner movie comprised of the intensity he wanted to play at and the runs he wanted to make. Actions that would give him the best opportunity to score.

We can only guess the images Rooney creates in his mind as he prepares himself for a match. What internal movies do you think he has? Imagine you are Rooney and you are preparing to play for Manchester United tomorrow. What would you picture? Have a go. Perhaps it goes something like this:

"Goals. Ball comes to me, lay it off and run in behind. Shots away, left foot, right foot. Busy around the box, non-stop work, make a nuisance of myself. Always looking to break the opposition line, get between the 2 center backs. Press them, make them feel uncomfortable. Draw defenders out of position – give my team mates a chance to score. Find impossible to mark position – lively, on my toes, push through to 95 minutes."

Picture this scene through the eyes of Rooney. Wear his red shirt and compete with his intensity and desire. Be Wayne Rooney in your mind for 5 minutes.

*The will to win is shadowed by the
will to prepare to win*

David James

If there is a lonely role in the team game of football it is that of the goalkeeper. The nature of the position brings with it the burden of outcome. In any other place on the field you make a mistake and you can very easily get away with it. Make one as a keeper and it is likely you become the villain.

The goalkeeper requires a great mindset. He must command from the penalty box and organize his back line with efficiency. He can see what others can't - so he must be the eyes for his team mates who don't always know the danger is coming. His awareness must be impeccable. He is the last line of defense and also the first instigator of attack. He must be brave. He must jump higher, stronger and with greater timing than everyone else when a whipped crossing ball threatens his goal area.

At 6 foot 5 inches former England goalkeeper David James is the perfect specimen for a shot stopper. But for the 41 year old who, at the time of writing is yet to retire, a career between the posts has never come easy. He struggled to settle at the world famous Liverpool Football Club and was told to "*Stop moaning and get on with it*" by coaching staff when he asked for help with his performance mindset. James looked elsewhere for his mental work freely admitting that visual imagery has become a mainstay of his performance and preparation.

"I imagine the ball coming towards my bottom right-hand corner, and see myself catch, parry or punch it away. Then I go through every variation of that shot and save. Game days are a classic. I wake up in the morning, get breakfast or whatever, jump in the shower and then just stand there for 10 minutes going through it. Then, in the car, I stop at the traffic lights, catch a few crosses and go on. When my team-mates are up the other end of the pitch, I'm busy visualizing what might take place." (Source: The Guardian 22/5/04)

Just like Wayne Rooney, David James mentally immerses himself in a world of competition on a daily basis. He leaves no stone left unturned by trying to picture every eventuality a match might bring. His mental rehearsal is just as important to him as his physical training.

"Clean sheet. Dominant in goal. A brick wall – the penalty area my home. This is my area and I dominate it. Flying saves, a touch to everything. Vocal with my back line – command with no let up. Crosses no problem – always safe. Catch cleanly every time. One versus one I love. Good technique – set, hands high, take."

These inner pictures and movies reinforce your soccer image and create a fortress around your self-belief. They drive your performance confidence for the upcoming match. Commit to this process every single day. Commit to thinking like a winner.

To win you've got to be confident. To be confident you have to think like a winner. It starts with thinking

What are you rehearsing?

Players such as Wayne Rooney and David James innately understand or have learnt that they need to nourish their mind with thoughts related to how they want to play. Whether by design or not, they take time during their day to mentally predict a successful soccer future.

All too often when a soccer player thinks about his future soccer, whether it is related to the immediate game or the season ahead, he thinks about how he *doesn't* want to play. He runs plays in his mind related to losing the ball, missing and getting beaten. This is because our brain finds it easier to register, remember, and think about negative events more quickly and deeply than positive ones. This is why Elvis from the previous chapter found it so difficult to recall his great games. He bookmarked his failures while he lost the mental page of his Under 21 match for Latvia against Romania when he had performed so well.

Elvis remembered the goals he let in while he forgot the saves he had made. The brain is better at rehearsing failure. A leading neuropsychologist called Rick Hanson calls this the "brain's negativity bias". He says that the human nervous system scans for, reacts to, stores, and recalls negative information about oneself and one's world. I love the way he describes the brain as like Velcro for negative experiences and Teflon for positive ones. What I don't love is that this means the brain's natural state is to shatter a positive soccer image.

Players like Wayne Rooney and David James are fantastic athletes with a great deal of footballing ability but at the elite level they will be subject to the same kind of mistakes amateur soccer players make. Rooney will give the ball away, miss an easy tackle and fumble great opportunities to score. Let's face it - he has far more pressure steeped on him when he plays! He carries the weight of 70,000 supporters at Manchester's Old Trafford stadium and the burden of having to please millions of Manchester United supporters around the world, from the U.S. to Japan. He makes a mistake and the whole world is watching. And yet he doesn't dwell on this burden of expectation. He chooses to imagine success. He chooses to create a stadium in his mind and run through the game he intends to play.

What are you choosing to rehearse in your mind? This is an important question because, perhaps unbeknown to you, your brain is rehearsing all the time and influencing your soccer image and how you *feel* about your game.

Work on your confidence and you may just be more skillful than you'd ever thought you'd be

The Brain is always switched on

The brain is a constant never-ending cacophony of noise. It simmers away out of sight all day every day. If I was to open your brain I would be confronted with electrical activity similar to looking at an electrical storm on earth from space. The brain buzzes as the billions of brain cells connect and reconnect. Even a resting brain, your brain when you're chilled out, is alive and active.

This constant commotion means that the brain is always switched on. It is sorting the receipts of your soccer pictures even when you're not consciously aware of thinking about soccer and it is developing what it thinks are the most appropriate soccer images for you.

Have you ever found yourself sitting around watching a bit of TV or playing a video game when suddenly some thoughts about your football pop into your head? This is your brain prompting you about your game. It is reminding you of the important skills you need to execute to play at your best. The challenge is that the brain is brilliant at reinforcing how you *don't want to play* rather than how you want to play. This process is part of the negative brain I describe above. Your challenge is to communicate with your brain to make sure it displays the very best pictures because it is these images that will help you and your body *feel* like you can compete at your best.

Questioning the game ahead

The game is on Saturday. It's Monday and I'd like to know what you are you feeding your soccer image because what you tell your soccer image will make a big difference to how you feel come match day. Are you doing your best game drill? Are you honing your memory by thinking about your best games? Have you opened your Soccer Bible today? Do the positive confident words you've written down dominate the pictures and movies you hold in your mind? Are you immersing yourself in a world full of soccer self-belief?

Let's take things further. Let's crank up the work you're doing on your soccer image: time to start using your imagination.

As a football psychology consultant my work is more question than statement. Most of the sentences I form are completed with a question mark rather than a full stop or exclamation mark.

"Do you think the way you were talking to yourself helped you?"

"Will the attitude you have in training today take you where you want to go?"

"What specifically did you enjoy about last week's match?"

These are just a few of the questions I ask my clients every day. By asking them questions I give them an opportunity to look into a different world, where their thinking and behavior is slightly different and so can produce different results.

I want my clients to mirror this questioning for the simple reason that I want them to use their imagination. I want them to think about what is yet to come. I know that if my clients enjoy the process of asking great questions they will cultivate a strong soccer image and enjoy the benefits of a mindset full of self-belief.

This is because I know that when they answer the questions they ask themselves they open up a bunch of pictures in their mind. And these pictures drive their soccer image. This is exactly the same for you. Ask yourself a question about your soccer game and in the process of answering yourself you will send a number of images into your conscious mind that feed into your soccer image.

Words create your pictures. Your pictures drive your self-belief. Your self-belief drives your confidence. But it starts with your words

So what questions can you ask yourself that feed your soccer image for the games ahead? Here are a few examples:

- *What will it look and feel like if I play my very best in the next match?*
- *What movement will I have if I'm dynamic, on my toes, and fully aware of what is going on around me?*
- *What will the crowd see if they watch me score a goal?*

Try this out right now. Ask yourself something about your football related to your next game. Make it a positive question because you want to drive positive, upbeat images into the forefront of your mind.

"What will the coach see the next time I score a goal?"

"He will see me start to make my run down the middle of the pitch as the ball goes out to the left wing. He will see me get across my marker by moving left then right. He will see me time my jump perfectly and meet the crossed ball with a powerful header. He will see the back of the net bulge as the ball dives past the

keeper's outstretched arms. He will see me celebrate."

One question, lots of *exciting* pictures. Lots of pictures to boost your soccer image and self-belief for the upcoming game. Lots of images that force home how good you really are. Lots of images that spread a feeling of certainty through your body.

There are a limitless number of questions you can ask yourself about an upcoming match. The primary goal is to open up a catalogue of pictures and movies that help reinforce you at your best.

Questions allow you to exercise your imagination and take ownership of your thinking and your soccer image. Questions help you direct your brain in the right way. You become the boss. Rather than being a slave to the negative statements that pop into your head - asking questions is a proactive form of thinking. Questions enable you to come up with responses and thoughts that take charge of the pictures and movies that take center stage in your soccer image.

Belief isn't a quality that is switched on easily. It must be massaged every day through great inner pictures and movies

A Secret: The Mind's Body

Close your eyes and picture your favorite footballer. Now picture a loved one. Finally, picture the street you live on. These kinds of pictures activate parts of the brain involved in visual perception.

Now I'd like you to imagine yourself kicking a ball. Look down at the ball and feel yourself swing your leg, make contact with the ball and kick through it. In this task you are using your mind's body, you are actually feeling the actions in your body. It's the same as imagining you are writing something or drawing a picture. Imagine kicking your leg, waving your arms in the air and nodding your head. Psychologists call this *motor imagery*. What is important for you to know is that during this process you are feeling the action of the movement you are picturing.

Like psychologist William Straub, another leading American brain scientist called Alvaro Pascual-Leone found some amazing results when studying visualization and performance.

Pascual-Leone asked students to do an experiment where they had to do a five fingered exercise. He had 2 groups: 1 group who physically did the movement and a second group who weren't allowed to actually 'do' the exercise. They had to imagine themselves doing it instead.

The students in the 2nd group spent 2 hours a day, 5 days a week, picturing their fingers moving in the sequence asked of them. The key, Pascual-Leone explained to them, was to make sure they *felt* the movement of the fingers as they imagined them actually move.

The results of the experiment were incredible. Pascual-Leone used modern brain scanning technology to examine the brains of the students after they had completed the task. He discovered that the brains of the group who had simply imagined doing the task had changed in the same way as the brains of the group who did the task physically.

Amazingly just by imagining the movement - the brains of the students had changed.

The brain changes with everything you do and anything you think about. This is why it is so important to think about how you want to play (rather than how you don't want to play). Think about heading the ball with strength and it changes your brain to make this more likely. Think about checking your shoulders and the brain becomes structured to help this to happen. These blueprints on your brain help you to see the game as full of possibilities rather than full of potential hazards.

The brain cannot tell the difference between what is real and what is imagined. This statement lies at the heart of sport psychology and is so important – it is worth repeating. *The brain cannot tell the difference between what is real and what is imagined.*

As you live your inner pictures/movies the secret is to bring as much action to the visualization as possible. *See* yourself compete and *feel* the movements - the motion and the actions that are relevant to what you are picturing. In this way you will re-organize your soccer brain and build a strong soccer image.

Don't just see yourself making a run – feel the running. In your mind, kick your legs as fast as you can. Feel your head swivel as you look over your shoulder to see the ball in the air. Feel yourself stick your foot out to control the ball and feel the ball land softly on your foot. As you go on a long mazy dribble feel the ball tap the inside or outside of your boots as you see yourself take players on. Feel their bodies barge into you and feel balance and strength as you maintain the steadiness of your feet. As you strike a shot feel the weight of your body behind the ball and the power dispersed onto the ball.

The more you *feel* as well as *see* the more powerful your imagery becomes – the more your brain changes toward the soccer brain of your dreams.

Bend your Imagination

The great thing about your imagination is that it doesn't have to reflect reality. No matter what your standard of play you can build a football world in your mind that goes beyond what you would ordinarily think is possible for your game. You can see and feel yourself scoring world class goals. You can see and feel yourself playing in a cocky manner with your head up, picking perfect passes time and time again.

Why not be a little outrageous with your inner movie? Why not imagine that in your next match as a defender you will win every header and every tackle? As a midfielder why not picture completely dominating the middle of the park: delivering dead balls with precision, dribbling through a cluster of players and spraying accurate passes out to the wings. If you're a goalkeeper enjoy the feeling of making point blank saves and jumping high above the opposition to catch and claim the ball. As a striker embellish your scoring movie. See and feel the ball come to you on the edge of the area and feel a perfect strike on the ball as it powers its way past the goalkeeper.

Switch on automatically

Asking yourself questions can act as a useful guide to envisioning the images you want. But you don't have to. The human mind has the capacity to picture things at will. Do so now. Picture your soccer.

You see? Easy. Easy because as a baby this was your main form of thinking. It was only when you went to school that you learnt to put letters and words to pictures of things in your head.

But please don't concern yourself if the images in your mind are a bit scratchy. Not everyone finds it easy to see their internal pictures and movies with real clarity. That's okay - it doesn't matter. Just by getting a fuzzy image you will still be exercising your brain – you will be firing the areas in your brain that relate to your soccer performance.

Of course with time, patience and practice your images will get clearer. Just keep trying to make your images big, bold and bright. Relax, don't force things and play football in your mind.

Make an Imagination Home

Recent psychology research has shown that teenagers who live close to places where alcohol is sold are more likely to engage in underage drinking. Research has also shown that over-eating is as much to do with the things around us as it is to do with hunger. For example, the bigger the plate - the more you will eat. The bigger the spoon - the more dessert you will eat. Have chocolates in the cupboard and you'll eat them.

Our environment shapes us. It doesn't just shape our behavior but also our thinking. The best soccer clubs in the world have great facilities, not just because they know that players need all the right training equipment to be physically and technically prepared. They understand that if players *think* they are the best prepared team then their self-belief will grow.

My challenge to you is to create an environment where your imagination can thrive.

Choose a location or place where you are quite often on your own. It might be your car, your bedroom or a study. You might choose to pick a specific place such as a room you go into a lot at school or at work. It could be a place in a park you often visit to chill out. I want you to make this your 'imagination home'. Every time you visit this place I want you to fill your mind with pictures and movies of you playing at your best in your upcoming matches. Ask yourself the questions you think are most important to you and allow your imagination to run free.

See how you want to play before you play...
then trust your vision

Sell Your Game

Every day you are sold to. On every TV, on every high street, in every cinema and in every magazine. On a daily basis you are bombarded with messages from retailers telling you how great their product is. They won't stop. It's relentless and will remain so for the rest of your life.

Tomorrow you will see some adverts in print or on screen. It may be from the Coca Cola company telling you how thirst quenching and fun it is to buy their drinks. It may be McDonalds reminding you about how great their burgers and fries taste. Or it may be the Mercedes car company relaying how safe and smooth a drive their vehicles give their customers. They will be selling and re-selling to you tomorrow and the next day and the day after that because they want to stay high on your mental map of the world. They know that if they stop showing you their goods, and how great they are, you'll go cold on them, ignore them and look elsewhere for similar products.

The focus of your mindset and the content of your soccer image is the same. You need to sell yourself to yourself. You need to direct your soccer image not only toward what you do well (your memory) but also toward what is going to go well. Build a commercial/advert of your future success. In it show your soccer image exactly how you intend to play. Make the advert big, bold and bright. Be a great salesman. Show off your skill and confidence on the ball. Demonstrate mastery in movement: how you find space and move into it, and how you make runs for your team mates to spot.

Adverts are memorable. Make yours one to remember.

Use Your Soccer Bible

Your Soccer Bible is an ideal place to store all the questions you have that help you open positive pictures and movies. Take time to write them down. You want to be able to come back to them every day.

Your imagination is a powerful piece of software that your brain's computer uses all the time. I strongly advise you to use it wisely. Condition yourself to enjoy envisaging how you want to play rather than how you don't want to play. Your brain is brilliant at directing you toward the negative but be proactive with your mindset. Ask yourself great questions and I promise your brain will offer pictures of you at your best.

Taking control of your memory and imagination will supplement the technical and physical work you are doing on your game by helping you assemble a positive soccer image. By starting (and sticking!) to these mental techniques you are committing to having a confidence regime. Matches in football come thick and fast so keep believing in yourself. Keep remembering your best games and stay committed to imagining playing how you want to play. Now let's take further steps toward controlling your thoughts and feelings related to your football. Let's play the perception game.

4

The Messi Mindset

He was offered his dream on a paper napkin.

It was Carles Rexach, the Barcelona Sporting Director, who scribbled his future on it and handed it over to him. That first exchange was to change the course of history for the Catalan club and for the 11 year old boy who was the recipient of the casually written contract.

This now well told story heralded the arrival of the boy from Rosario, Argentina into Spanish soccer. At the world famous Catalan club he was to hone the ability that had shone through while playing in his native country.

Lionel Messi had shown incredible talent while competing for his hometown team and then at Old Newell's, a Rosario professional club. He would often take on 3, 4 and 5 players before passing or getting tackled. His ball control, balance and co-ordination were something to behold and have been shown the world over on documentaries about his life.

His talent is undeniable but so is the ability of many young footballers when they start out on their journey to stardom. They don't all become stars and they don't all become as good as Lionel Messi – the man who has taken up the crown from Diego Maradona as the World's greatest soccer player in a generation. Many disappear into the shadows of club soccer. To my mind Messi is Messi because he has more of the attributes of a champion than everyone else. The building blocks that make up his performances are higher and stronger. Some of these blocks relate to his mindset: his mental attitude toward football and toward his life.

"Something deep in my character allows me to take the hits and get on with trying to win."

Here he is talking about being tackled, making no fuss, getting up, maintaining confidence and getting on with the game with the same will to win as before. It is certainly a positive reflection on his performance toughness. But I think this quote is more of an insight into his general mentality and a clue into what has made him the player he is today.

To my mind it is Lionel Messi's *perception* of every situation he experiences that has had as much an impact on his status in the world game as his raw talent has. When you add a positive mindset to hard work and talent - you have a soccer cocktail primed for success!

A soccer player should ignore anyone who says he can't

Impossible is Nothing

"When I was 11 I had a growth hormone problem. But being smaller I was more agile. And I learnt to play with the ball on the ground because that's where it felt more comfortable. Now I realize sometimes bad things can turn out good."

Messi said this on the iconic Adidas 'Impossible is Nothing' adverts and it gives us a great insight into his mindset.

As a boy he was nicknamed "La Pulga" (the flea) because of his height. But it appears Messi cared little about his stature and brushed off suggestions that size would prevent him from playing as a professional in the future. His *perception* of the situation was helpful, positive and above all confident.

Messi refused to let his physicality handicap him. In fact he used it to his advantage. "*I am more agile,*" he said. "*I can learn to play with the ball on the ground better than everyone else.*" I believe, despite the fact he was smaller, he *felt* taller than his teammates. He may have physically looked up on everyone but he chose to mentally look down on his opposition. He cared little for their body shape. He only thought about his soccer, his ability, and how he wanted to play.

A footballer should never allow herself to be in awe of another player.
Respect yes, but in awe, no!

The situation is the situation

The third form of thinking that drives your soccer image is your perception: how you *see* every given situation. This is a form of thinking that could also be described as your attitude. How you react and respond to events as they happen.

Essentially you see things in one of two ways: positive or negative. I know that the idea of 'positivity' strikes fear into the heart of some people so if that's you - then feel free to use alternative words if you want. You might use helpful or unhelpful, constructive or destructive, upbeat or downbeat as opposed to positive or negative.

Whatever words fit your preference I hope you agree that your reaction and responses to things are important. If, after being dropped from your football team, you react and respond in a negative, unhelpful, destructive or downbeat way this will damage the great soccer image you are developing. A negative perception feeds your soccer image pictures of you being unable, incapable and helpless. If you let in an easy goal and respond negatively and unhelpfully ("*I can't believe I let that one in. I'm an awful shot stopper*") then your soccer image will keep reminding you of this by sending you pictures of you being an awful shot stopper. You will damage the belief you have in yourself as a goalkeeper as well as lessen your confidence to save and block shots on match day.

In contrast, positive responses and reactions maintain strong soccer images. They build the belief you have in you, and magnify your confidence for your upcoming fixture. I think we can agree that Lionel Messi perceives things in a helpful and positive way. He refused to allow his growth hormone problems to get in the way of his footballing development. In fact he made his height work for him. This approach helped him feed his soccer image - the idea that 'he can' and 'he will' no matter what.

I want you to understand that perception is a *choice*. That your situation is your situation and it is how you *choose* to react and respond to the circumstances that count.

If you've spent the whole match missing sitters and easy chances - you get to choose your perception on the team bus home. You can choose to think unhelpfully about your game *"How can I have missed so many chances. I looked stupid in front of everyone out there"*. Or you can choose to think in a helpful way *"Not my best day in front of goal but it happens to all the best strikers. I need to look toward doing a bit of practice in training then be more positive with my shots in the next match."*

A champion is brilliant at *seeing* the events that happen to him in the most helpful and positive way he can. He omits the word 'problem' from his dictionary and emphasizes the word 'challenge' on a daily basis. How you see the challenges you face on and off the football pitch shapes your soccer image and subsequently reinforces your self-belief and confidence levels. You have to take control of your perception.

Belief develops from hard work, quality work, great visualization and great thinking

The Neville Challenge

The positive perceptions of former English footballer Gary Neville helped propel him to legendary status at one of the world's leading clubs. A man who would openly admit to being of average talent - Neville grew up playing at the Manchester United Academy amongst some of the best modern day players in England. He played alongside a young David Beckham, a youthful Paul Scholes and a fresh faced Ryan Giggs. These 3 players would go on to define one of the most successful teams Europe has ever seen. But Gary played in that team. He qualified not through God given gift but through hard work and great thinking; through an unrelenting positive perception of his situation.

As a young full back at the Academy he looked around and saw some seriously good talent. He had a choice - he could choose to dwell on this as a negative or look on it as a positive situation. He could choose to *see* it as impossible to progress amongst a group who were the best of their generation, or he could *see* the situation as full of possibilities. He chose the latter.

He chose to think about how lucky he was to be able to compete against some of the best young players on the planet. He chose to think about how good he could become if he worked harder than them. He chose to imagine the exciting future he would have if he used them to help him learn about his role as a full back quicker than other young players who played in the same position. He chose to look at the situation in a positive light and it paid off. He didn't moan and groan; he didn't give up.

Did Neville always shine at the Manchester United Academy? Of course not! You can be assured that at times the passing of Scholes and Beckham caught Neville out. But he knew with training he'd learn to read their passes and with practice he'd adopt a better position to intercept or clear their balls. Similarly I'm sure that if you'd had the fortune to watch the United Academy players train in the early 1990s you would have seen Ryan Giggs pull a trick or two and ease his way past Neville on the left side of midfield. But I trust that Neville, with his patience, persistence and positive perception slowly learnt how to deal with wingers with pace. He didn't panic. With every one versus one against Giggs he was able to study his body language, the subtle body movements that helped Giggs twist and turn his way past players. Neville soon learnt what body shape to adopt, where to look, when to hold back and when to tackle. With a positive perception his skill levels developed.

Neville grew a strong soccer image because he exhausted his mind with positive pictures and movies allied with a never-ending desire to work harder than his team mates. His soccer image thrived and he was able to deliver a robust response when the public said he wasn't good enough to play for England. Because he had spent his formative years nourishing his soccer image with an 'I can' and 'I will' attitude, his soccer image returned the compliment by feeding him a 'never give in' mindset when the world around him said he couldn't. But he could, and he did! He became Manchester United's club captain for 5 years and the most capped England right back ever.

Is it any coincidence that with such tough minded individuals in their team Manchester United was arguably the top club in Europe (perhaps the world) by the end of the 1990s and into the 2000s. Gary Neville was a standout example but he wasn't the only mentally fit player in that team. Let me take you back a decade and tell you the story of David Beckham.

 No-one's thoughts are purely positive. A soccer player must learn to be aware of his negative thoughts then be able to let them go

David Beckham

The breaths helped him stay composed. But the eyes told all. They were a window into the pressure he was facing at that exact moment in time. The weight of a nation rested on his shoulders or more accurately relied on the curvature of the flight of the ball.

This time he had to get it right. If he did, all would be forgiven after that villainous night nearly 4 years earlier. The England team was playing Greece and only needed a draw to qualify for the 2002 World Cup. With 89 minutes on the clock they were losing 2-1. David Beckham stood 10 yards back from the ball and lined up a free kick that could send his country to the World Cup and rebuild his reputation with the England supporters. He started his run up...

David Beckham was vilified for several years in England because of a rash moment in the heat of battle. During England's 1998 World Cup game against Argentina, Beckham kicked out at Diego Simeone and was sent off. England went on to lose to their South American rivals leading many to blame Beckham for his moment of madness. The next few years led to obscene chants from the terraces, death threats, and constant negative press stories.

"You will go through tough times, it's about coming through that."

There is no brilliance to Beckham's words but they are neatly in line with the philosophy I believe is so important for all footballers to adhere to. Was it easy for Beckham to set foot on a football pitch in front of 30,000 fans every week chanting his name in a derogatory way? No! Was it easy for Beckham to feel comfortable in an England football jersey again? No! Was it easy for Beckham's career to implode? Yes! But it didn't. His perception over his career has been exemplary:

"I will make mistakes but I will keep practicing."

"I will have poor games but I will keep trying to put in positive performances."

"I can't control what others think of me but I can work hard and be the best person I can be."

David Beckham is famous for his free kicks but I'm sure a statistician can show that he has missed more than he's scored. He fails at them more often than he succeeds. When he misses a few in a match does he stop the daily routine of practicing free kicks? Does he think to himself *"I can't believe I missed a couple today. I'm getting rubbish at them. Time to let someone else take the free kicks?"* Or does he think *"So disappointed to miss a few today. Not my normal high standard. Better go and practice tomorrow and score one next week?"*

Beckham knows that according to the law of averages he's going to miss quite often. He knows that being human he's going to make mistakes on and off the pitch. He knows he can't control everything. He certainly can't control what people think of him. This iconic figure chooses to perceive his soccer game in the most effective way possible.

David Beckham scored the free kick against Greece. He sent me and millions of England supporters into raptures. He received a standing ovation in the press room (from the harshest of critics.) He won the public back and his perception continues to deliver success.

 Confidence and attitude are everyday things. They can never be perfected... but they can be nurtured

Chapter 4

'Stuff happens' – The Ultimate Soccer Image Maker

Goalkeepers fumble shots, defenders become distracted and leave a man unmarked, midfielders hit misplaced passes and strikers miss glorious chances to win in the last minute. If mistakes like these didn't happen - soccer would be a predictable and dull game. *And it's going to happen to you.* It is likely you will get dropped. It's probable that you'll have a beast of a training session some time this season and get a grilling from your team mates and the coaching staff. It's probable that you'll fall flat on your face and embarrass yourself. I won't be surprised if you go on a losing streak. It might be this season where you'll lose a few and you might get the blame for some of those losses.

I'm not being negative. This is how the game works: with inconsistency, with peaks and troughs, and with highs and lows. In response I'd like you to adopt the mindset 'stuff happens' (a slightly less blue version of the American 'sh*t happens').

The philosophy 'stuff happens' relates to an acceptance that there are things that happen to us that aren't particularly nice, or in our best interests, but they do happen. When you embrace this approach you will relax your immediate reaction to events as they unfold. You will see a situation with greater clarity and you will keep your feelings in check so you can assess matters rationally.

An uptight, anxious reaction will be accompanied by negative thoughts which in turn will only serve to assemble a negative soccer image. Having a mindset dedicated to the acceptance that 'stuff happens' will calm your response and give you the opportunity to perceive things in a helpful, positive and constructive manner.

"I missed some great chances today but stuff happens. I know I'll take those chances next week."

"Some of my passes were way off line today and I'm disappointed that Coach had a real go at me. But stuff happens and I have to keep working on being more aware of where my team mates are."

"I can't believe I've been dropped. I don't feel that's fair given how well I've played lately. Oh well stuff happens and it's up to me to work harder to win my place back."

*It is emotional toughness that is the next frontier
in player development in football*

Did I have fun?

Whenever I deliver a presentation to the parents of young footballers who play at academies or in youth teams my first message relates to what they should say to their young soccer player after a training session or a game.

Quite often well-meaning parents offer advice when they don't really know how to coach soccer themselves, or they offer encouragement. Being positive as a parent is of course very welcome and more often than not the correct approach to take after a young soccer player has experienced a poor game or session. But my presentation to parents gives them some alternatives and I want to share with you the most powerful question they can ask their child; a question that you can ask yourself after a training session. This idea is something you can use to help your perception of your game or training session in a positive way whilst remaining focused on learning and improving your game. So here, very simply is *the* main question you should ask yourself after a training session:

"Did I have fun?"

I hope I don't sound too much of a psychologist by saying that fun is a precursor to excellence, to success, to learning and to positive perception. There are very few athletes on this planet who don't have fun while in the process of becoming a champion. If you want a short cut to becoming a better footballer - have fun. Aim to have fun in every training session and in every match.

Fun brings with it freedom, expression and certainty; key skills to help you learn, develop and play at your best more consistently. Having fun means that making mistakes are annoying but fixable - they aren't permanent scares that will prevent you from progressing your game. Having fun means looking at your training and game experience in a positive light, even when others may want to remind you of things that went wrong. And having fun means getting the most from your time with your team mates. It means there is no blame and there are no excuses.

If you want to keep a positive perception while learning quicker and performing more consistently - strive to have fun on the pitch. Enjoy!

Talk rather than listen to yourself

I can't remember where I first heard the statement 'stop listening to yourself, start talking to yourself' but it's true. Boy is it true. As has been discussed, our brains tend to deliver a lot of negative thoughts into our conscious awareness. And we tend to listen to them.

"There is no way we're gonna beat this team, they're top of the league."

"I don't fancy my chances of scoring today against those massive center backs"

"I had a nightmare last week. I don't feel confident at all"

We tend to listen to these destructive, unhelpful perceptions. And we tend to let them dominate our feelings. We let these perceptions bring us down by making us feel worried and full of doubt and anxiety.

Champions are champions because they choose to ignore this rubbish the brain comes up with. In fact they drown out their negative self-talk. They stop listening to themselves and constantly talk to themselves.

"If we play together we'll have a good chance to win. They may be higher than us in the league but we've won tough games before."

"The center backs are big but if I use my movement and my pace they are playable. I just have to be more alert and more aware of my team mates and try to find space more often."

"Last week has gone. How I played has nothing to do with this next match. Train hard tonight and I'll play hard on Saturday."

There is no magic or secret to this. It's very simple. Just see the situation slightly differently, use a different voice and take time to summon up positive pictures and movies and you'll maintain a great soccer image. You'll feel good. You'll give yourself the best chance to perform at your best come match day.

If a footballer makes thinking her greatest strength, her greatest friend...then consistency of performance will be with her...always

Be your own Biggest Fan

Have you ever monitored what you've said to yourself during an average day? Have you ever paid attention to that little voice inside your head that directs you through your daily routine? Try it sometime; you might be surprised what you hear.

I read somewhere that 66% of what we say to ourselves is negative. I'm unsure if this is true but it certainly falls in line with how our brain is designed (the 'negative bias' that I talked about in the last chapter). What I do know is that I wouldn't dream of speaking to people how I speak to myself sometimes. If I did it would surely obliterate my social diary!

To listen to football fans is to listen to extremes. They are passionate about their subject matter but passion brings with it exaggeration. In favor players are outstanding, brilliant and unbelievable. They can do no wrong. They should be first on the team sheet. Out of favor players are terrible, awful and disgraceful. They can't do anything right. They should never play and if the manager dares to play them then he doesn't know what he's doing either.

I get this. I understand that in such an emotional sport where games are won and lost on the percentage, the inch or the single seconds then supporters will express emotional views that will change depending on the result of their team or the performances of individual players.

I think a fan's view on soccer is similar to the inner voice we all have. It reflects the up and down nature of life. We can have a great morning but a lousy afternoon. We can be told how wonderful we are one minute then how rubbish we are the next. There is no consistency in our environment so it is a real challenge to think consistently. But this is what I'm asking you to do. I'd like you to try and keep a positive inner voice no matter what the environment is laying on for you. Of course I'm not talking about times in life such as bereavement or other such circumstances where people suffer the misfortune of personal tragedy. Soccer never has been and never will be life itself.

I believe that if a footballer can have an inner voice that reflects the views of their biggest fan then he will improve his soccer image. If you don't have a 'biggest fan' then make one up. If you've had a bad training session what would your biggest fan say to you? If you've been dropped how would he pick you up? If you feel you've not been playing to the best of your ability what would your biggest fan remind you of?

"Your think you were rubbish today but you weren't. You played some great through balls and made some crunching tackles."

"Remember how good you were last week in the match. Everyone thought you were man of the match. You were outstanding."

"I don't care what anyone says - you are the best on this team. If you keep working hard you will be player of the year."

This is the voice of your biggest fan – always seeing the positive even when there are plenty of negatives floating around. Your biggest fan helps you perceive things in the most positive and helpful way possible. If you find yourself plunged into a world of negativity bring out your inner fan. Allow him or her to absorb you back into a world of 'can do'.

Keeping it real: Learn to Flip

I have quite a few people say to me: *"But I think about the bad stuff because I need to be realistic. I need to learn from them. If I haven't played well then why should I say I've played great? That's not true, it's not fact."*

The problem with this way of thinking is that you will constantly bombard your soccer image with the bad stuff. You will bookmark failure. Your mistake list will grow bigger and bigger. By being 'realistic' and remembering the mistakes you made and the poor parts of your performance you have no chance of building your self-belief and confidence. And by being 'realistic' I assume people mean feeling down or giving up on the art of good thinking: *"Well that was a rubbish game for me and no one can tell me any different. It just wasn't good enough."*

Being a realist is nice but that mindset doesn't create a champion. A champion tends to be a mindless optimist

I have some sympathy for this attitude. I never want my clients to settle for second best or for average. But win or lose - your game is rarely subject to fact. A striker can have a great game yet score no goals. A keeper may play a blinder yet lose 5-0. A midfielder may have a pass completion rate of 98% yet play against a team enjoying 75% possession.

Self-belief and confidence require you to be a positive perceiver of your soccer and this means you have to think helpfully every day, after every training session and after every game… even when you've lost 5-0 and you've been told you were horrendous. That is the skill in the process. That is when I really help my clients.

This is the challenge I set my clients and the one I want to set you - when you think about your football you must spend at least 80% of your time thinking positively, what your strengths are, what you did well, and what works. 20% of the time you must analyze what needs to go better. And then you have to flip the weakness. By 'flip' the weakness I mean see the weakness in a positive light.

Let me give you an example. You take a little time to think about your last match. You decide you gave the ball away too many times. You decide that your weakness is your passing. Now you flip the weakness. You need to say to yourself: *"Great, I'm going to work hard on passing. I'm going to work so hard that it's going to become a strength. How exciting is that, my passing will be a strength."*

After letting a striker get in front of you a few times leading to several goals - flip what happened: *"Not my best day but it highlights how hard I have to work on reading the movement of the striker. If I add that to my game my defensive play will be really solid. Training is tonight, I'm going to start working on it then."*

After being man marked out of the game - you flip what happened: *"That center back was so strong today. It shows how much I have to learn about the art of forward play. I can get goals but I can get another 10 or more a season if I become a little more intelligent with the runs I make. I also need to be more agile. Improve the 2 together and that center back will have no chance next season."*

After being dropped you flip this disappointment: *"I just have to work harder and better. I don't know why I've been dropped so I'm going to speak with the coaching staff. It will be a good time to get them to assess my game and come up with a few solutions for me to improve."*

An interesting fact about champions in any sport is that they dwell on their strengths but they acknowledge their weaknesses, what is working and what needs to be better. And they love to work on and improve these areas in their game. They are students of their sport, in their own mind taking playing qualifications every time they step out into the arena.

Inside you must believe you are the best soccer player. Outside you must learn from others every single day

Injury time

The half time whistle is about to blow. The last 3 chapters have been dedicated to help you think in a way that feeds your soccer image pictures and movies that help build a strong self-belief. Let's take half time to sum things up.

Half-time

The half-time whistle has gone. Time for refreshments and a team talk, or in our case - a summary of the concept of self-belief and details of how to build it. Brief and easy to understand team talks are the most effective so let's keep this short and really simple.

If you want to have a lot of performance confidence going into each and every match you have to have a strong and resilient belief in yourself.

Champions are champions because they have a great deal of self-belief. They are high in this mental quality because they are not only great physical specimens and great technicians but also great thinkers. Their superior thinking helps them build a strong self-image specific to their sport. So, Sir Chris Hoy (three times Olympic champion) has a strong cycling image. Kobe Bryant has a strong basketball image. Roger Federer has a strong tennis image. I'd like you to build, develop and maintain a strong soccer image – how you see yourself as a soccer player.

Your soccer image (and subsequently your self-belief) is influenced by three forms of thinking:

- Memory
- Imagination
- Perception

Memory

To start with, champions are particularly skillful at remembering the good times – the times when they have played at their best. The brain loves to hone in on times when you've failed (remember, it's warning you *not* to play like that again but in doing so spreads pictures of poor moments of play across your mind). Champions are brilliant at shining an attention light toward matches and training sessions that won them praise from coaching staff and fellow team mates.

What are you remembering about your football – from last week, from last month and from last season? What are you remembering about your play from your training sessions and your matches? What comments are you remembering and what plays are you putting to the forefront of your mind?

I work hard with my clients to help them direct their thinking so they remember their best games and their best moments. Just by writing down on a piece of paper (or hopefully in your Soccer Bible) your three best games in detail and looking at your words every day, you will feed positive inner pictures and movies into your soccer image.

This doesn't mean I want you to ignore your weaknesses. Excellence requires a long look at what you don't do well enough on the soccer pitch. But I want you to put these weaknesses into perspective. I want you to get enthusiastic about improving them and excited that doing your hard work will add extra dimensions to your game.

Imagination

Champions are champions because they envision success. They use their imagination to shape their future – short and long term.

Great footballers take time every day to picture how they want to play in their upcoming game rather than how they don't want to play. They are accomplished at ignoring the prediction of failure that the brain loves to settle on, and they open up a catalogue of positive pictures by being proactive thinkers.

Do you imagine success in your next game and for the next season? Are you proactively thinking by asking yourself positive questions? Asking an upbeat positive question such as "*What will it look like if I dominate the pitch in my next match*?" will guide your mind to play clips of you on top form and will inject your soccer image with confidence.

If you want to feel truly confident going into your next match - allow your imagination to settle on the goals you want to score, the passes you want to execute, the saves you want to make, or the clean sheet you want to have. As you picture a dream game use all of your senses as vividly as possible - *feel* the bodily movements that are involved in the action sequences you picture. You don't have to be realistic with your images – bend your imagination. See and feel the unlikely, the extraordinary, and the impossible. This will add to your soccer image and your feelings of confidence.

Perception

Are you going to have a brilliant soccer image if you react to a poor training session in a moody fashion? If you think about yourself as a terrible striker following a goalless match are you going to send waves of belief through your body? Are you continuing to manage your soccer image effectively if you argue with your manager for being dropped?

Your soccer image is also driven by your perception - how you *see* every given situation.

The manner in which you react and respond to everything that happens in your soccer on and off the pitch is not only a crucial life skill but also a crucial determinant of your soccer image. Perceive things in a negative way and you damage your soccer image. Find ways to see things in a positive light and helpful way and you will continue to develop a world class soccer image.

Thinking is a choice, so whether you respond positively or negatively, helpfully or unhelpfully - thinking is under your control at all times. It's not always easy to respond in the most appropriate way, one which positively reinforces your soccer image, but it is without doubt vital to do so.

React and respond in a negative way and you will play football in a world of unhelpful emotion, poor focus, less motivation and reduced confidence.

Like all my clients I want you to become expert at reacting and responding positively, helpfully and constructively to every given situation. The referee made a poor decision that led to your goal being ruled out? That's fine, decisions balance out in the end. You had a shocking game and might get dropped as a result? That's fine it's time to work harder and address your weaknesses. The opposition are the strongest in the league? Excellent, now there's a chance for you to shine in a tough match.

Find yourself talking to yourself negatively? Think everything is unfair and against you? Stop. Do what Lionel Messi and David Beckham did? They looked at their tough situations and made their circumstances work for them. They continued to enrich their soccer image by thinking effectively about their circumstances.

The Second Half

Time to get back out there and show them what you're made of.

You've got techniques and thinking philosophies to build your soccer image and subsequently your self-belief. Now it's time to explore ways to play with confidence and focus, to train effectively, and to build a growth mindset. Keep an open mind and keep moving forward.

5

How Richard Developed his Focus

It was the words on the blue flag that gave him an injection of confidence, even a big hit of belief.

He saw it as he was tracking back, as he was making sure the strikers didn't get in behind the back line. The four words emblazoned on the flag said "In Keogh We Trust", a message that 'said it all' about the battling full back. It was held aloft by supporters of his team - Carlisle United - reinforcing the commonly held view at the time that this was a defender going places.

He was a strong traditional full back – far too good for the league he was playing in. He was great in the air, hard to beat on a one-versus-one, and he possessed a sound positional intelligence that made it hard for the opposition to get around him.

It wasn't long before bigger clubs came knocking and just over a year after he had absorbed the positive messages sent to him from the stands at Carlisle he won a transfer to English Championship team Coventry City.

Life sometimes takes a turn of luck and I felt that way when I received a call from my friend Cos Toffis. Cos, who is Richard's agent, explained to me that Richard was passionate about developing his game and would welcome the opportunity to meet and discuss the finer elements of performance mindset. I jumped at the chance. That phone call allowed me to enter the football life of Richard John Keogh.

The Soccer of Richard Keogh

As a soccer psychology consultant most of my life is spent fixing problems. Unsurprisingly I am rarely called in because a footballer has scored a hat-trick or has just made his debut for his national team. My presence is mostly required when something is missing or lacking in a player's game and the coach or player himself has decided it is mindset where the problem resides.

With Richard, however, things were a little different. During our first session it soon became apparent that he was one of the rare breed of soccer player who wanted to see me because he wanted to explore ways to become better: to be as good as he could be. Rather than asking for something specific to be fixed, he merely wanted to develop new playing philosophies and techniques that could help him maximize his career. He longed to play in the Premier League and he wanted to win international caps for Ireland. He just wanted to improve.

After a short discussion about his strengths and weaknesses we felt that Richard's main challenge was to improve his performance focus on the pitch. We agreed this would afford him the opportunity to deliver a game with greater consistency. Lapses in concentration had seen him make a few mistakes the previous season, mistakes that were holding him back from receiving attention from even bigger clubs. We agreed that performance focus was a muscle in his mind that needed building. He was hungry for success so we got to work straight away.

Focus in soccer is vital. A player can be immensely talented, have great technique and yet his career may falter due to poor focus

The Premium Skill

I remember the first ever meeting I had with a football manager. He told me that if I helped his players improve their focus he would use me as his soccer psychology consultant for the rest of his working life. He put the skill of performance focus on a pedestal and explained to me that the small mistakes made by footballers often stem from a lack of focus - from switching off - for a few vital seconds.

Having now worked in football for many years I couldn't agree more with this manager. Performance focus in football is vital – a little like the importance that a steering wheel has to a car. You can have the self-belief and confidence (the engine of the car) but without the necessary focus and concentration on the pitch (the steering wheel) - a footballer's game will be erratic and inconsistent. A player can be immensely talented, have great technique, and yet his career may falter due to poor focus.

Lose performance focus and you can lose your technical game and tactical execution. Switching off leads to mistakes, to indecision, to a lack of awareness and to slow anticipation. Take your mind off the game for a second and you can cause an array of problems for yourself and your team mates. Switch off as a defender and the opposition striker can nip in front of you and get a shot away. A distracted midfielder won't see the runs of his team mates or the movement of the opposition. An unfocused striker will fail to find space or lose his marker. Goals will be in short supply!

The soccer player who tends to give in to distraction cannot respond appropriately to the demands of the game. For me more goals are conceded due to lapses in concentration than for any other reason. And more games are lost due to players switching off for a split second than for technical or tactical mistakes. Lost focus means a failure to take opportunities. It enables the opposition to get to the ball first. It causes sloppy free kicks and spilt crosses at vital times.

The soccer player who tends to switch off cannot respond appropriately to the demands of the game. He will think slowly & react slowly

The Focus Secret

In football, it's not about having *more* focus. It's not about going into some deep trance state. In football it's all about where you *place* your focus.

This was my first message to Richard. I wanted him to understand the good news that the best soccer players don't have some Zen like focus that mere mortals can't aspire to. They are simply skillful at directing their focus on the most appropriate things during a game. These are things that help them execute their technique and tactical game plan to the best of their ability.

When a soccer player switches off, to my mind he is not shutting down his focus. He is merely switching his focus to the wrong thing. So a defender might focus on the ball too much rather than focusing on both the ball and the man he is marking. This isn't a lack of focus rather it is a focus in the wrong direction. Similarly a goalkeeper might focus on the crowd of players in the penalty area on a crossing ball while a more useful focus would be on the ball itself. A striker might focus on his marker rather than on space to move into, while a midfielder might watch play on the left side of the pitch so losing awareness of the run the right winger is making.

It's not just things external to you, such as the ball or the opposition, that can destroy performance focus. A footballer may be *too focused* on his inner voice. He may be talking to himself about the mistake he made 5 minutes before or how long there is to go in the game. If he's focused internally on either of these he won't be focusing on the tasks he has to execute in the game.

Richard understood what I was saying to him – that performance focus is about directing your focus of attention correctly. To give him a deeper understanding I asked him to complete a short exercise that I'd like you to do now.

The myth of focus is the concept that more focus is required. It is placing your focus in the right direction that is a crucial mediator

Focusing on what can be controlled

What from the list below can *you* control? What can *you* only influence? And what can *you* NOT control at all? So to clarify: that's control, influence, and cannot control.

- The weather
- The result
- The referee
- Your thoughts
- A mistake you've just made
- Ball control
- The state of the pitch
- You scoring a goal
- How long there is to go
- Jumping high
- Winning a header
- Work rate
- The opposition

Just like all my clients Richard found some of these easy to categorize while others made him think a bit. I'm sure you found the same. Let's categorize them together, starting in reverse order with what you can't control.

Can't Control

- The weather
- A mistake you've made
- The state of the pitch
- How long there is to go

There are probably quite a few factors in there that may have surprised you. The most obvious ones are the weather and the state of the pitch. It's fairly evident that you can't control those aspects. And yet how many soccer players place their focus on them? Many times I've walked onto a pitch with the team before a game and heard someone say "*I can't believe how bad the pitch is. How can we play well on this?*" Where do you think this soccer player's performance focus is going to be during the match? Do you think he might be easily distracted?

Similar to the state of the pitch I've heard footballers moan about the weather. Last season a player came up to me on Thursday and said he hoped it wasn't going to be raining during the game on Saturday because he had decided he was rubbish when playing in the rain. I, of course, pointed out that if he wanted a career in professional football in England he was probably going to have to get used to playing in the rain (it rains a lot in England!). Joking aside do you think this player's thinking going into the game was helpful? His performance focus was inevitably going to be damaged if it rained - something he couldn't control.

This struck a chord with Richard straight away. He mentioned another aspect that can affect performance focus – whether you are playing home or away. He mentioned that whilst he was able to focus, irrespective of where he played, he felt that in past teams he had played with team mates who focused too much on the location of the game. An away match meant they 'tried not to lose'. They played on the back foot. They played to avoid mistakes - a negative mindset as a result of an inappropriate performance focus.

Influence

- The result
- The referee
- You scoring a goal
- Winning a header
- The opposition

Winning, keeping clean sheets, and scoring are a few examples of performance focus that, at first glance, appear positive and productive. A champion should have an enormous will to win; a goalkeeper should hate to concede and a striker should love nothing more than popping the ball into the back of the net. I cannot argue with those performance philosophies and I too yearn for victory just like everyone else. But these damage your performance focus. You can't control winning and a focus on wanting a particular result just works to distract you from your tasks in the game. Focusing on winning can make you nervous: "*I don't want to lose*" can become your mantra. The result, and winning, will take care of themselves when you focus on the correct things.

Whilst you cannot control the referee you can certainly influence him. But focus your mind on the referee and you take your attention away from your game. The same can be said for the opposition. You cannot control the opposing striker as a defender but you can influence him (hopefully to play poorly). Similarly you might think scoring a goal is completely within your control. It's not. Going into a game with a mindset attached to scoring can damage your performance thinking. If the clock is winding down and you are yet to score you may start to panic. Equally a mindset obsessed with scoring can make you nervous and tentative. It can make you worry and doubt yourself.

Richard had always approached a game with a focus on not conceding, or to put it more positively, keeping a clean sheet. But as we went through this task he realized this could be a damaging thing to focus on. He couldn't control keeping a clean sheet and in previous games he'd allowed himself to feel down when his team had let in a goal, even when he had nothing to do with the goal. He realized his performance focus had to be better directed.

Playing without care of outcome is preferable to
caring too much

Control

- Your thoughts
- Ball control
- Jumping high
- Work rate

So here are the things you can control from our original list. And these are perfect things to focus on.

I asked Richard if he could control his thoughts. He agreed he could. I asked him if he could control what he was saying to himself on the pitch and whether he could control how he reacted and responded to events on the pitch. Again he agreed he could.

I also asked him if he could control whether he jumped with strength and could control the level of his work ethic. His answer was a straight-to-the-point *yes*. Provided he was fit, of course, he could control those two things.

I explained to Richard (as I would like to explain to you now) that whilst you can't control winning headers you can control jumping high with strength and with dominance. You can choose to think positively, you can choose to look in a certain direction, and you can choose to work as hard as you possibly can in that last lung-busting 10 minutes of time. It's tough to do but it's a choice.

I told Richard that he needed to focus his mind on the things that he could control at every given moment on the pitch. This would allow him to completely ignore what he couldn't control.

"I can't control the pitch, I can't control where I play, and I can't control what has happened five minutes before."

I explained to Richard it was important for him recognize what he could influence but that he shouldn't dwell on these things.

"I want to win but I understand I can only influence winning. I can only influence the referee, I can only influence scoring a goal, and I can only influence keeping a clean sheet. These can't be controlled... only influenced. Recognize them but don't dwell on them."

I want you to understand that the only thing you control on the pitch is you - you control you. Your performance focus needs to be on you or related to you, not to anyone else, nor to an outcome such as scoring or winning.

Having an awesome performance focus every second of the 90 minutes you play means ignoring what you can't control. It means growing the skill of recognizing but not dwelling on the things we can only influence. And it requires a mind that focuses tightly on yourself, on doing the key habits that will help you to be the best individual you can be, and the best team mate you can be.

"I can control what I'm thinking in the 1ˢᵗ minute, the 40ᵗʰ minute and the 80ᵗʰ minute. I can control the actions I take and the way I react and respond at all times."

The time in the match is irrelevant. So are mistakes just made. Control the controllables

John the Striker

Some of my clients like to work in private with me and don't wish to be identified. One such player was someone I'll call John. John was (and still is) an English Premier League striker. A very good one in fact! He is very famous and has played for his country many times.

As all elite sports competitors experience at some stage in their career - John was going through a bad patch when I was asked to do some work with him. He was a regular goal scorer but his goals had dried up lately. He hadn't scored in a few months and not only was the press suggesting that his career was over but his own fans were starting to get restless during matches when he was missing chances to score.

The message from everyone around him before every match was this: *"You've got to score. Today you've got to take your chances"*. Team mates were telling him how important his goals were and that if he kept playing games without scoring then the team would continue to suffer (the team were slipping down the league at this time, adding even more pressure on John). Others tried to be positive: *"You're going to score today - I can feel it. It's going to be your day"*.

The communication from those around John was damaging his performance focus. During a match he was so focused on scoring that he started to panic in front of goal. Instead of being patient he became rushed, snatching at shots leading to poor contact or inaccuracy. And because he was so obsessed with scoring he started to forget his other duties as a striker. The manager had to constantly remind him to defend from the front (especially as a few goals were conceded that could easily have been prevented by John pressing and closing down the opposition defenders).

I've worked with many strikers and many go through the challenge of not scoring at some stage during their career. And John was no different to many of the others. I had to deliver one consistent and vital message to him every single day: "*Stop focusing on trying to score goals. You cannot control scoring. Stop listening to those people who tell you that you have to score. You cannot control scoring. Start focusing on the things you can control – the things that will help you to score. In this way you will give yourself the best opportunity to score. In fact scoring will then take care of itself*".

This was an important message for John because he had to understand that he couldn't control scoring – that a performance focus on scoring was damaging to him because it would harm his mindset. I wanted him to acknowledge that on some days defenders will have a great performance and mark him out of the game. On other days the goalkeeper will have a world class match and save everything John throws at him. John needed to relax and accept that the ball wouldn't always run for him and the more he focused his mind on scoring - the more pressure he heaped on himself.

At first John didn't get this but as more scoreless games came and went, and the more we talked, the closer John got to the correct performance focus. He started to understand that he could only *influence* scoring. He could only execute the things that would help him to score. That's all.

Your PFC

Allow me to introduce you to the bit of kit that manages your soccer performance – the Pre-Frontal Cortex or as we'll now call it: the PFC.

The PFC is the part of the brain 'where it's at' - when it comes to your soccer performance. It sits just behind your forehead and is the part that helps you think, focus, plan, make decisions, recognize patterns, interpret, manage emotions, and it also plays a big role in muscle coordination. That's a seriously heavy job the front brain has. It manages and controls the skills that are vital to football. Your ability to execute your technical, tactical and physical skills is largely determined by this part of the brain.

Now here is an interesting problem. The PFC is tiny. In fact it's minute. It runs out of gas and switches off easily. To give you an example - think about a time when you were in the middle of doing something and someone asked you a question that required you to stop… and think. You had to stop what you were doing because you were using up space in the PFC and there was no more room. You had to stop and free up space in order to think of the answer to the question you were asked.

Chapter 5

Players can't help but be distracted at times...it is the way the brain is designed. But they must deal with distraction...quickly

When the PFC switches off it becomes harder for your body to perform the skills you've trained so hard to improve. It's tougher to spot the runs of your team mates or notice gaps to run into. It becomes harder to make quick decisions. Your emotions become less easy to ignore and the simplest of passes can go askew as you find it trickier to focus on your team mates.

By focusing on the things you can't control you fill up the area of the brain that manages your performance. Factors such as the weather, the mistake you made, the fact you're a goal down – they all help to overload your PFC. They leave less room for the important tasks your role in the team requires of you.

I explained to Richard that he needed the PFC to stay switched on every game. As a full back he needs the PFC to remain switched on to keep anticipating the runs the winger he marks makes. He needs the PFC switched on to work out the body shape he needs at any given time to get the best view of the movement of the opposition. He needs the PFC switched on to time his jumps to win his aerial battle against his opposition.

If you are a striker you need the PFC switched on to make the right runs, to find space, to pull away from a defender, to time a shot that's been passed across the penalty box. You need the PFC working correctly to be able to see space, to act on that information and to control the ball when it's slotted through to you.

As a goalkeeper you need the PFC switched on for you to make the decision to come for the crossing ball. You need the PFC operating at full power to anticipate the direction the penalty will be struck. And you need the PFC switched on to command your defenders at all times.

As a midfielder you need the PFC functioning to decide the best ball to play at any given moment. You need the PFC switched on to win your tackles. You need the PFC to help you get box-to-box and to link up play with the strikers.

You know about winning

The PFC is a vital piece of kit that must be handled with care. It is the engine room of your game intelligence and the crucial juncture where mind and body meet. By having a performance focus directed towards the things you can't control, or the things you can only influence, you are feeding it unnecessary information.

You already know about winning. You know you want to win. You know you want to score and you know as a defender that it's ideal to keep a clean sheet. So stop filling your PFC with the stuff you can only influence. Influence them by focusing your mind on the things you can control.

If you arrive at your match and the pitch isn't very good - ignore it. Avoid letting a bad pitch fill up your PFC and damage your performance focus. It will slow you down and destroy your vision and movement. If you're playing away from home - ignore this fact. The pitch, goal posts and ball don't know you're away from home. Respond to the location of the match by focusing on what you can control.

Ignore the referee. He may make some decisions that frustrate you but don't give the opposition the upper hand by allowing refereeing decisions to fill your PFC. Allow the referee to carry on with his job while you carry on with yours.

I knew that Richard could direct his focus away from the things he couldn't control and by doing so it would contribute to him winning player of the year at Coventry City. I also knew that if I could give him a simple focus philosophy he would clear his PFC and play with greater awareness and anticipation improving the great defensive skills he already had. So we quickly got to work on a new way of focusing: the me, the now, the script.

6

Your Match Script

I believe the great ones - no matter what their sport or their industry - begin with the end in mind. They see in their mind's eye how they want to be in the future. They envision their perfect self. They picture their destination.

I have an end in mind, a dream if you like for all my clients when it comes to performance focus. Some of my dreams go like this:

Jane tackles the striker which the referee sees as a foul. Jane believes it was a fair challenge but gets up and quickly runs back to her position. She focuses on what she can control. She finds the person she's marking quickly and instructs others to do the same.

John breaks free just inside the penalty area and lashes at the ball. His shot blazes wide of the right hand post. He goes to put his hands on his head then catches himself. He focuses on what he can control. He gets his head up and runs back into position ready to win the ball again.

Jake keeps losing headers to the man mountain center back who towers above him. But he loves focusing on the only thing he can control – himself. He maintains his confidence though and works on different ways to win the ball. He uses his body effectively and tries to tire the center back by constantly moving. He keeps going.

Sarah knows that time is running out. Her team are one nil up in this crucial cup game and she can see her team mates desperately trying to play the game out.

She knows she can't control the clock - just her game. She ignores the time and absorbs her mind on the things she can control to give herself the best opportunity to keep playing well.

My *end in mind* is for my players to play with a mindset that focuses tightly on the elements of the game they can control. In my vision of their ideal future they ignore the things they can't control and only acknowledge what they can influence. Their soccer minds and performance focus are wrapped up in the things they can control. There is nothing outside of this bubble. They adhere to this rigidly and with discipline.

This was the vision I had for Richard Keogh. I wanted Richard to fall in love with the performance philosophy I introduced to him. I wanted him to be *the me, the now, the script*. In this way he would get the very most from the great ability he had. It would give that extra few percent that would help him deliver week in week out.

A player must play with intention. He must play with anticipation & forethought. He must play with will and skill and want

The me, the now, the script: a focus philosophy

These days I work solely as a soccer psychology consultant. This wasn't always the case. When I finished playing professional golf I took up coaching the technical side of the game. And after completing a degree and Master's degree in psychology I went on to working with golfers on their mindsets. Much of what I learned in golf I use in soccer. Of course there are many differences in the psychology of the two sports but there are some commonalities too.

I have found the performance focus of golfers and footballers to be quite similar. The bad shot into the water that led to a double bogey tends to linger in the mind of the golfer just as the mistake that led to a goal will stay with a footballer as he competes. The golfer can get wrapped up in how his opponents are playing. The soccer player can focus too much on the quality of the opposition. The golfer can focus on irrelevant things unrelated to his swing. A soccer player can focus on the ball too much.

Whilst the two sports work at completely different speeds (as well as one being an individual sport and the other being a team sport) it is performance focus that forges a link between the two. And it was while I was working with golfers that I came up with a mantra that I feel is not only relevant for football but for all sport no matter what the nature of the game. The mantra is *the me, the now, the script*.

The Me

There is only one thing on the pitch when you play football that you can truly control. That is you.

"The only person I can control on the pitch is me."

If I was to magically develop some soccer talent from somewhere and set foot on a soccer pitch I would place my focus on me. I would understand that it is only *me* that I can control and I would set out to manage myself: my reactions and my responses, my technique, my game plan and tactics, my role and responsibilities.

I explained to Richard that focusing on *the me* doesn't mean he should completely ignore the opposition, the referee, his coach, the crowd and his teammates. I told him focusing on *the me* would help him focus on the things he could control and help him deal effectively with the things he could only influence.

During my first season working with Richard he played predominantly as a full back. He played against some pretty good wingers and strikers – players such as Scott Sinclair for Swansea, Max Gradel for Leeds United, and Craig Bellamy for Cardiff City. As a new player to the English Championship division it would have been easy for him to place his focus on these players. It would have been easy for him to start dwelling on the pace of Sinclair, the energy of Bellamy and the skill of Gradel. This performance focus would have gotten Richard down. It would have suppressed his game.

For Richard to give himself a chance to play well for 90 minutes he had to stick to *the me*. He needed to have an inner voice that said *"Come on, stop focusing so much on him and start focusing on me. Come on, focus on me"*. In this way he could be the best he could be in that game. By switching his focus onto *the me* and then by thinking in a confident and helpful way he would give himself the best opportunity to deal with the toughest challenges (and the best players) on the pitch.

I wanted Richard to adopt *the me* - an acknowledgement that he was playing against a great winger but a mindset that dwelled on the things he could control. I'd like you to enjoy playing with the same performance focus. I'd like you to play *the me*. I challenge you to ignore what you can't control, acknowledge what you can influence while immersing yourself in *the me*.

By all means tell yourself that you want to win. But remind yourself that if you dwell on the outcome during the game you might start to panic. If the score remains nil-all for most of the game or if you go a goal down and your focus is on winning you might start to get anxious.

"I want to win but I know that I will give myself the best opportunity to win if I focus on what I can do. Stay focusing on the me."

I understand that it's important for you to pay some attention to the opposition during the game. That goes without saying. But the correct focus on the opposition is one that simply notices *what* they are doing rather than *how* they are playing. A quick judgment of their strategy is all you need then you must switch your focus back to you.

"This winger is using his pace to go round me on the outside. No problem, I'm going to show him inside."

"The defender is trying to outmuscle me. No problem, I'll get a little sharper with my movement and roll him."

"The midfielder is playing balls in behind the defense. No problem I'll make sure I read a ball played to him earlier and get tight to him quicker so he has less time to line up the pass."

In this way you are briefly acknowledging what the opposition is trying to do but you are re-focusing back onto you quickly. There is no inner dialogue dedicated to how well the opposition is playing, how good they are, and how they are bound to beat you.

Avoid a performance focus on what you can't control, acknowledge what you can influence and dedicate your mindset to focusing on *the me*.

The Now

Can you change the mistake you made five minutes ago? Can you take back the ball you gave away that led to a goal against your team? Can you re-attempt the sitter you missed in the first half?

A footballer can't change the past, nor can the manager, and even a psychologist can't roll back time.

"I can't change the past, I can't control the past."

It's the same on the soccer pitch as it is in life. A soccer player must commit himself to letting go of the past during a match. When he does he will give himself more chance of playing with freedom and with precision.

Likewise it's easy to get ahead of yourself and look to the future during a match. Projecting yourself to the future during a game is a focus destroyer and a waste of energy.

I asked Richard if he could be tuned in and focused on his responsibilities when focusing on how long there was to go in a game. I asked him if he felt he would be able to play with freedom if he was worrying about something that hadn't happened yet. I asked him if he felt he was able to read the game and anticipate appropriately if he spent time re-running in his mind the mistake he'd made five minutes before.

I told him that a future focus while playing was a negative performance focus - concentrating on your worst case scenario, *"What if they score?"* I explained that this performance focus prevents you from playing your natural free flowing game - the result will be to play within yourself because your focus of attention is on avoiding mistakes. Ironically this type of focus increases the chance of you actually making mistakes - it increases the likelihood of the situation you *don't* want to happen.

Letting go of the past and avoiding a focus on the future during a match helps you escape the mental prison of past action and prediction of what is yet to come. This prison slows your anticipation and lessens your movements. It fills up your PFC and switches off your capacity to be aware of what is going on around you. A player who is truly in the now plays every few seconds as they come. He ignores the past and removes his mind from the future.

I know great players like to think ahead, players like Xavi Hernandez and Andres

Iniesta. But when they talk about future thinking they're not referring to 5 or 10 minutes later. They're talking about 5 or 10 seconds. They're focusing on pulling defenders away to make space for their team mates. They're focusing on finding positions where they can be passed to. They're predicting the imminent runs of the strikers who play in their team.

To me an optimal focus is on *the now* – this means the present moment and the next 10 seconds. Anything outside of that bubble is irrelevant – not worth thinking about, not worth focusing on.

Playing in *the now* or *playing present* (another term I like to use) is one of the most basic and simplistic concepts I teach. Yet it seems to be one of the toughest to pull off. The soccer brain loves to predict ahead or put right what you've done wrong in the past. It wants that final whistle to come when you're winning and it likes to remind you what you've done badly as you compete. It's almost as if it's saying to you "*Don't do this again*".

I wanted Richard to understand, just as I want you to appreciate, that mistakes will happen on the pitch. You will misplace a pass, you will concede a sloppy goal, you will miss great chances to score and you will mistime tackles. No matter the error or blunder you must keep playing with a focus fixed firmly in *the now*.

Don't be a slave to the future. It will happen. Stay in the now. The outcome of the game will be resolved so stop thinking about it and place your focus in *the now*. If you're not having your best game - wanting the show to be over won't help. Place your focus in *the now* so you can take a little time to trouble shoot – to find a solution that will fix your game.

A player can be plagued by a wandering mind. The past is gone & cannot be controlled. The future can only be influenced by focus on the present

The me, the now: partners in performance focus

Richard loved the idea of playing *the me, the now*. He understood that by simply saying to himself "*the me, the now; the me, the now*" it would trigger his performance focus to tighten its attention on himself and the present moment. It is the perfect antidote for a mindset that likes to put too much emphasis on the opposition or onto past mistakes.

Of course he understood that this didn't mean he should ignore the opposition. To him it just meant that he should acknowledge the winger he was marking, take note of how the winger was trying to play against him, and then direct his focus to the things he could control to make it as difficult a game as possible for the winger.

I advise you do this in your game. I believe you will play at your best if you stay in *the me, the now*. By managing your performance mindset and keeping it firmly within the boundaries of *the me, the now* you will find it impossible to play and compete with doubt and worry. As a goalkeeper playing in *the me, the now* it will help you to come and claim crosses without the burden of worrying about other bodies in the box. As a defender you will profit from *the me, the now* – it will keep you alert, alive and ready to cut out through balls and block spaces that opposing strikers may have spotted. As a midfielder in *the me, the now* you'll benefit from the freedom this mindset gives you. Pinpoint passes will be your forte. The striker who plays *the me, the now* just keeps playing no matter how many chances he has missed. He doesn't dwell on the sitters, he just keeps striving to deliver the shot that will win the game.

The great footballer carries on. He misses, he carries on. He gives the ball away, he carries on. He goes a goal down, he carries on.

Chapter 6

The Script

As has been discussed - staying in *the me, the now* isn't easy. It's a simple concept but not easy to apply. Fortunately this performance focus philosophy has another level – another step that enables a footballer to play with the right focus.

The next step is to develop what I call your match script. Your script is 2 or 3 plays you want to execute during the game that are plays you can control and are related to your role and responsibilities and your mindset.

Let me give you some examples:

- Non-stop movement
- Win my headers: time jumps
- Push winger on the outside at all times
- Work hard – box-to-box
- Talk to myself confidently at all times
- Focus on me
- Be strong in every challenge
- Be dominant on a crossing ball

I can't emphasize enough the importance of the two characteristics of the plays that make up your script. They must be things that you can *control*. This means they must relate to you as you are the only person you can completely control. If you look at the list above you can control all of those plays. You can control having non-stop movement, you can control timing your jumps, and you can choose to work hard. The second characteristic is just as important – plays must be related to your role and responsibility, or to your mindset. Again these are things you can control.

I'd also like to see the plays in your script expressed in a positive manner. Avoid the word '*don't*' – as in "*don't challenge weakly*" or "*don't concede fouls*". Not only are these statements negative but they also use the word don't. The brain doesn't recognize the word don't. When you say "*don't look behind you*" what do you want to do? Most likely you want to look behind you. When a coach says "*Don't foul*" what as a player does that make you want to do? Yes, it makes you want to dive in and tackle someone in an unfair manner.

Let's take a little time to note down some more plays that might make up your script. Remember, they must be written positively (what you *do* want to do) and should be related to your role and responsibilities and mindset.

- Stay on my toes at all times
- Be vocal: loud for 90 minutes
- Check shoulders more: at least 10 times a minute
- Track the runners: defend the back line
- Make runs behind the defense
- Look up and relax when I receive the ball
- Hold the back line – push everyone up when the ball is cleared
- Press high when we don't have the ball

I always recommend having 2 or 3 plays but you can have just 1 if you want. I would advise you to not have more than 4 otherwise you will overthink things on the pitch. I also don't think it advisable to have a script that involves plays to do with technique. I believe it's important for a soccer player to trust his technique as he plays.

Trust is a vital ingredient in excellence because overthinking leads to a rigid and anxious execution of body movements. Imagine thinking about where you plant your feet as you walk up the stairs. If you do so you'll likely fall over. Technique should be practiced on the training pitch. That is the time to think about where to place your foot when you control the ball, or what body angle is best for you to hold the ball up. The training ground is the place to work on the intricacies of ball strike and head placement as you take shots. On match day a trusting mentality is required. If you mis-kick or sloppily lose control of the ball avoid critically analyzing your technique – leave this to the training ground.

Having a script with plays related to technique will likely fill your PFC. Remember we are trying to engage the front brain, not fill it up.

There is nothing more destructive than dwelling on mistakes. This focus merely compounds the initial error

Chapter 6

The striker script

A recent session with a striker led to these 3 plays:

- Non-stop movement for 90 minutes
- Get in the box: Be a constant threat in the area
- Stay upbeat no matter what happens

This was a Premiership striker and an example of how the script doesn't need to get any more complicated. This is a perfect script to help this striker stay in *the me, the now*. The plays were relevant to his role and appropriate to the responsibilities his coach had given him.

He wanted a movement play to remind him to work hard off the ball, because this was when he tended to score - when he worked hard. This was also when the manager praised him most - when he worked hard for the team. The second play required him to get into the box more and make a nuisance of himself in the area. When he did this he gave himself a great chance of finding space and scoring. His third play reminded him to stay positive at all times as he tended to get a little down after mistakes or when his team went a goal down.

The midfielder script

This script is taken from a session I did with a midfielder who played in the top division in France:

- Close down quickly when my opposite number gets the ball: unsettle him
- Look for diagonal balls to the left wing: exploit their slow right back
- Be constantly vocal: intimidate with my voice

These 3 plays were a nice balance of responsibilities on and off the ball. Being constantly vocal helped him to be a great team mate (by informing others of what's going on around them) and also helped him to stay switched on.

The defender script

This script helped a League 1 player (the third division in English football) win man of the match.

- Command with my body language: positive and upbeat at all times
- Talk to defenders non-stop: keep them aware of dangers
- Strong challenges: focus when tackling

The defender was a veteran player who felt he could allow the tactical side of his game to happen naturally, so he chose mindset plays. His body language and communication plays allowed him to be a leader, something he felt comfortable doing. He wanted to remind himself that this was his role in the team – he wanted to make sure he got that right. He also knew he was going to be up against quick strikers so he knew that placing extra emphasis on timing his tackling was important. He expressed this by having a play related to focus – *focus when tackling*. This script worked – he really was the best player on the pitch.

The goalkeeper script

Finally, here is a script from a goalkeeper I have been working with for the past 3 years. He has put together dozens of scripts in his time. This is one of them:

- Decisive on crosses: commit to fly
- Always switched on: keep moving even when ball is down the other end
- High hands on shots

You will notice a technical play (high hands on shots.) This is one of the rare times I allow this to pass. This goalkeeper regularly dropped his hands as he set his body to make a save. It was almost like a bodily trigger to prepare to stretch his arms out and the goalkeeping coach felt it was a very destructive technical error. So we decided that the keeper should have a play in his game that helped him to hold his hands up as he prepared to make a save.

Thinking in the moment under the lights in the heat of battle requires an open mind free from the burden of poor focus

But I Like To Play With a Blank Mind

Many of the coaches I talk with about the script refer to the concept of the 'zone'. They point out that a feature of this well talked about mental state is a clear, uncluttered mind. They argue that a soccer player should play without any thoughts running through their head.

I too believe that the brain and nervous system work best when a soccer player is merely playing and reacting instinctively to the challenges that unfold. Being intuitive, automatic and reflexive is a mindset and way of playing that all footballers should adhere to.

But to me the researchers who study the zone are not saying that there should be no thought. Simply there should be less thought. Perhaps that means having 2,000 thoughts pass through your conscious mind as you play rather than 10,000 thoughts. No one will ever know the exact amount of thought required to be 'zone-like'. What I do know is that players who set foot on the pitch with a match script have something to focus their mind on, as well as something to take their mind away from the things they can't control. And they have tangible, controllable things to come back to when they get distracted.

The script keeps the PFC buzzing rather than overloading. It paradoxically keeps an uncluttered mind by helping you to focus on the areas of the game that are important to you. With several simple plays within a basic script you give yourself a better chance of climbing into the zone.

An overly technical mindset on the pitch merely leads to an overwhelm of thoughts. You need to think a bit...but keep it simple

The me, the now, the script: a summary

Like all my clients Richard Keogh has a script for match day. Three simple plays that help him focus on himself, in the present moment. His script helps him run onto the pitch on match day with basic things to focus on. The plays help him ignore the things he can't control and enable him to avert his focus from the things he can only influence. Richard knows a great game will take care of itself if he executes his script. If he gets distracted he knows he has something to come back to – something to focus on.

Richard lets a great game take care of itself. He knows he can't completely control this. He can have a great game but the person he's marking might just be a little better on the day.

I'd like you to adopt Richard's philosophy. If you want to win the match, *focus on your script*. If you want to win your personal battle against the guy you're marking, *focus on your script*. If you want to score, *focus on your script*. If you want to keep a clean sheet, *focus on your script*. Your script drives your focus and subsequently drives your performance.

Sticking to *the me, the now, the script* is a challenge because the game brings with it not only opponents (and team mates) but also good and bad luck. Performance focus offers a rollercoaster experience. Especially given the way your brain is designed. As this next chapter will explain, it is your brain that can be your own worst enemy.

7

How Carlton Squashed his ANTs

I never saw a great Tottenham Hotspur side. Not like the great winning teams of the early sixties or the successful European team of the mid-eighties. I was a late-eighties and nineties fan and despite the enormous talents of players such as Englishmen Paul Gascoigne and Gary Lineker, Spurs never hit the heights of the wistful years gone by.

Despite their lack of success I grew up a fan of Spurs and never in my wildest dreams did I think I'd change allegiance. As all soccer fans know - it's not the 'done' thing. But when you work with soccer players or a soccer team your loyalty to your boyhood club becomes stretched and a meeting on the 1st of August 2007 was to change my feelings for my beloved Spurs.

My work with Carlton Cole of West Ham United saw me celebrate a goal against Spurs. It saw me jump with joy as my client left the Spurs defense shaking their heads in frustration. I had rebelled against my much loved team – but I was happy. Carlton Cole was making headlines at last.

Chapter 7

I'm Forever Blowing Bubbles

The first meeting took place at the Boleyn Ground Upton Park, home to West Ham Football Club in East London. Upon arrival I was escorted to one of the boardrooms that overlooked the pitch. I took in the view. It was a bright summer's day and the pitch looked immaculate just like the closely mown grass of a Wimbledon or Augusta National. However this grass hadn't graced the likes of a Roger Federer or Tiger Woods, but had enjoyed the stamp of equally compelling sportsmen such as the England great Sir Bobby Moore. Gazing out into the stands I imagined supporters in full voice singing the West Ham anthem: 'I'm Forever Blowing Bubbles'.

Fifteen minutes passed until a gentle knock at the door halted my gaze out the window away from the hallowed West Ham turf and back into the room. I turned to see my future. I turned to see Carlton Cole sheepishly standing in the doorway, or more accurately covering the whole of the doorway - a mountain of a man. My first thoughts betrayed me as a soccer psychology consultant. "Can this guy really have confidence issues? How has this guy not killed it in this league?"

I've heard psychologists say we make our first impression almost instantaneously. Judgment is determined by the clothes people wear, by their mannerisms, their physical appearance, and by how they speak to you. Sometimes we get this judgment wrong and I believe it is physical appearance that must be the prime cause of misjudgment. There are a lot of big guys playing football and it's so easy to think that because they are big they are bound to be confident, without fear and full of self-belief.

A polite if slightly timid Carlton Cole entered the room and greeted me with a warm handshake. We sat and talked.

The Story of Carlton

"Two years ago I watched Carlton play for the reserves and I saw two animals in him - one was a rabbit and the other a lion. I want to see that lion come out in him more often." Claudio Ranieri (former Chelsea manager.)

Carlton Michael Cole Okirie had been a star player in the youth team at Chelsea Football Club. He scored a bucketful of goals as he dominated defender after defender with his strength, height and skill. A sure thing for the future. Claudio

Ranieri - the Chelsea manager at the time - called him his lion and after Carlton scored on his first team debut the whole of England waited for him to explode onto the scene. But the eruption never happened and Carlton spent unsuccessful loan spells at Charlton, Wolves, and Aston Villa only to transfer to West Ham in the summer of 2006.

Carlton relayed this information to me as, being a psychology consultant, I always like to know a little about someone's past. It has always fascinated me that an individual with the ideal physicality and with talent to burn could fall so far from grace. Here was someone destined to be a superstar now languishing in the West Ham reserve team. How had this young soccer player gone from super hero to, if not quite zero then seemingly, soon to be zero? Where had his talent gone? Did his physicality in the youth set up mask poor technique or a lack of skill? I doubted that, and the word from the coaches that knew was that Carlton Cole was the real deal. He could own training. He could run the show. But on match day this Carlton, Carlton the lion, didn't show up.

Quick feet may be a physical phenomenon...but they soon become sticky when a footballer isn't equipped to perform under pressure

The great divide

It turns out Carlton was a victim of the *great divide*. That difference between the mindset one has on the training pitch and the mindset one has while performing in the pressure cooker that is match day.

I think the *great divide* has destroyed more promising careers in soccer than anything else. Having worked with a lot of youth team players at professional clubs I've seen a great deal of talent fail to materialize. Yes there are a host of reasons why but a recurring cause of failure can be laid firmly at the door of the great divide. Many young footballers with skill to burn are unable to overcome the uneasy feeling they experience as they walk onto the pitch on match day. It's this feeling - of fear, doubt, worry, and anxiety - that delivers sub-standard performances bringing with it enormous frustration for coaches because they see the same players stand out in training every day.

Chapter 7

The difference in feeling between training and playing can be enormous. Why? The way I describe it is like this:

Picture a piece of wood in front of you, a piece of wood about 30 feet long and a couple of feet wide. Do you think you can walk across without falling off it? Easy, right? Now let's change this simple challenge. Let's hoist that piece of wood 1000 feet into the air. Do you think you can walk across it now? The task is still the same. But what has changed? Your perception of the task that's what: "If I mess up I'm going to die." You'll probably get across okay, if you dare to try. And if you do - will you walk in the same cocky manner in which you walked when the wood was on the ground? Probably more carefully I would think.

Carlton Cole and thousands of soccer players like him can play in training. They play with intensity and focus. They demonstrate vision, alertness and competitiveness. They score, they defend and they tackle and harry their team mates. They can play seriously well. This is because it's easy, it's just football. Training is just having a 'game of football'.

But when it comes to match day suddenly they *have* to get it right. There is no hiding place. They feel they are being judged – by their coaches, by the supporters, and by their team mates. They wonder what people will think if they make a mistake. They question their ability. The fire that burns so brightly in training fades to smokeless rubble on match day.

Carlton found himself in this space. His debut game for the Chelsea first team went okay. But during this match he wasn't so much a 'rabbit in headlights' he was more a rabbit dashing across the road. He didn't think about the occasion, the stadium, or the opposition. He just got on and played in the way he did for Chelsea's youth team. But Chelsea was and still is one of the world's top clubs. To maintain your place you have to be one of the very best on the planet in your position. Carlton knew this and started to question his ability and his future. He soon forgot the dozens of goals he scored for the youth team. He didn't listen to the praise lauded on him by the manager, Claudio Ranieri. His only vision became one of him failing. His only voice became one of '*I can't*'. Negatives drowned positives.

And so his performances suffered. Chelsea decided he needed more game time (as he was rarely in the starting eleven) so they loaned him to Wolverhampton Wanderers, to Charlton, and then to Aston Villa. Carlton scored few goals and failed to settle at any of those clubs. Behind the scenes he really started to doubt himself. When he played in Premier League games he didn't feel comfortable. Yes, in training his game was sharp but in matches his play was unreliable. He searched inside and knew that he lacked self-belief and a feeling of confidence when he crossed the white line and took the pitch. But he didn't know how to change things. This was when I was called in.

A soccer player must exercise her free will.
Thinking is a choice, so she must choose to think
effectively at all times

ANTs

I told Carlton he had an infestation of ANTs. Not the small insects but Automatic Negative Thoughts (ANTs).

It has been said that we have 66,000 thoughts a day and two thirds of these tend to be negative. How that has been measured I don't know but I can imagine the figure is not far off. Carlton had a nest of ANTs. He had thousands of negative thoughts related to his soccer, every day. The previous few years had taken their toll and Carlton was teeming with ANTs that hampered his progress.

When Carlton sat with me he spoke about the ANTs he experienced on and off the pitch. He was continuously 'falling off the wooden plank' and he wasn't helping himself by being worried during the week and spending time doubting himself. No matter how much talent you have, and no matter how physically fit you are, when you immerse yourself in the kind of destructive thinking that Carlton had, then you are going to play bad soccer. Carlton had an infestation of ANTs and he had to deal with them.

The first few chapters of this book dealt with self-belief. Carlton and I worked on this area and on these techniques religiously. I knew that was the easy part. It was his on-pitch ANTs that were going to be difficult to squash. These were loud. They drowned out the positives and sunk any helpful thoughts that may have risen to the surface.

Chapter 7

It's all in your brain

I'd like you to do 2 short exercises. Let's do some clapping.

1. Clap for 5 seconds, 1 clap per second.
2. Clap 5 times for every 1 second. Do this for 5 seconds as well.

So why the clapping? The first exercise resembled soccer because to my mind soccer is played in seconds. It only takes a second to score a goal. It only takes a second to win or lose the ball. It only takes a second to deliver a free kick or corner. Soccer works in seconds.

The second exercise resembled your brain. As I mentioned in the introduction to this book your brain works in milliseconds. It works much quicker than soccer, in fact it trumps soccer for speed every single time. You have an immediate reaction in your brain to everything that is going on around you on the soccer pitch. The fact is, whether you like it or not, the brain is the quickest thing in all of sports.

So as you play soccer your brain works at lightning speed. In combination with this the brain loves to evaluate what is going on in its immediate vicinity. It enjoys assessing its close surroundings. And the challenge for you as a soccer player is that as your brain scans the game it loves to pick up on problems. It loves to attach itself to negatives. It hones in on the difficulties you are encountering.

Your brain is brilliant at focusing on problems as you play, such as refereeing decisions against you, a goal the opposition has scored, the fact you're playing against a man mountain center back, the mistake you made 5 minutes ago, the vocal support of the opposition fans, and the telling off you got from the manager 10 minutes earlier.

Make a blunder in front of goal and the brain will do its best to bring your thoughts back to this moment time and time again. It will throw ANTs at you in the blink of an eye. It will build an ANTs nest in your mind as you constantly picture the mistake you made.

"I can't believe I made that mistake. I've let my team mates down."

The ANT can be the brain's best friend (and worst enemy). Run onto a pitch at a venue where you've previously lost a couple of games and the brain will feed you an ANT.

"We always lose here. Not sure we'll be able to break that spell. I hate this pitch."

ANTs fill up your PFC. They load it up and cause it to malfunction and switch off. This in turn devastates your game intelligence. Tunnel vision will lessen your awareness of the plays your opposition makes. Your anticipation will slow as will your decision making. To the opposition you'll look slow, you'll look lethargic. Your individual performance shattered.

"We've got no chance today. This team are top of the league and flying."

"The manager is really getting on my back. I'm trying my best here...it's so unfair."

"This winger is flying. I can't get near him."

The brain works against you – it doesn't like to work rationally, it's just not designed to. It's a piece of hardware developed to keep us alive. It's no surprise the brain loves to throw ANTs at us. This form of thinking has directed you to safety your whole life. Because of ANTs you have learnt to be cautious in certain situations such as crossing a road or touching something hot. But the brain is lousy at recognizing what is a genuine danger to us. It thinks the opposition, the state of the pitch or the possibilities of a poor performance are legitimate dangers. It hurls ANTs at you so you play in a cautious manner. It wants you to play with too much care. It wants to slow you down, and yet slowing down can be the curse of the footballer.

Your ANTs need to be squashed – quickly and effectively.

It is speed of thinking that separates the greats from the goods. Speed of thought requires a clear, positive mindset

Squashing ANTs: SPOT STOP SHIFT

This is a very simple but very powerful technique I teach all my clients. But Carlton Cole really embraced this. It was this technique that was a big part of the process in going from reserve team player to England international. He used this week in week out in his matches in the English Premier League to make sure he was thinking effectively at all times.

SPOT

Psychologists always preach that awareness is the first step in change. I couldn't agree more - it's a real skill to recognize when you get a little negative on the pitch.

Soccer players tend to play on autopilot. Just as they are unaware of the physical habits they portray on the pitch they are equally oblivious to the mental patterns that underpin every action they take. Most soccer players compete in a state of blissful ignorance lurching from one negative thought to the next. A soccer player needs to develop the capacity to recognize how he is talking to himself. He needs to notice when he is thinking in a manner that is destructive to his game. Or as I like to say "*Spot the ANT*".

Building awareness of your inner football world as you play really is the first step toward mastering yourself on the pitch. Knowing what you are saying to yourself enables you to change your self-talk. You can start to take control of your thoughts rather than your thoughts controlling you.

Spotting your ANTs is more difficult than you may think. Largely because when you set foot on the pitch you are there to play football, not to analyze yourself. Analysis can and will get in the way so I always ask clients to start this process away from the pitch. Carlton was no different to anyone else I've worked with. I asked him to think about the thoughts he had in and around match day, before kick-off, during the warm up and as he played.

Have a think now about some of the negative thoughts you have. When do they tend to come into your mind? There is often a pattern to your ANTs. Maybe it's when you miss a few chances or lose the ball or go a goal down. Taking some time to think about when you have ANTs during the game can improve your awareness on the pitch. Write these down in your Soccer Bible – getting them out of your head and onto paper will help you tackle them more effectively.

A second step is to improve your awareness in training. Training is a time to progress your *spotting* ability. Whilst a practice session isn't the same as playing under the pressure a match delivers, it will still provide a fair reflection on when your ANTs tend to happen. A committed soccer player will always take a little time after training to sit down and reflect on the ANTs he experienced during training. He will regularly refer back to the ANTs he has documented in his Soccer Bible

At some point you will have to start improving your *spotting* during a game itself. This is tough - go easy on yourself. My advice is to have several in-game review moments and a half time analysis. There are always several down times during a game due to injury or when the referee is talking to a player. You may even get the chance when the ball goes out of play. Ask yourself *"What ANTs have I heard?"* You will have to be quick. Half time is a more convenient time to briefly run through the ANTs you've had. Swiftly note them and move on. You won't *spot* all the ANTs all the time straight away. This is a skill and it will take time to *spot* them all.

The faintest of touches can score a single goal.
The right thinking scores many goals

STOP

The next stage is to *stop* the ANT. *Spot* then *stop*! In other words your task is to *stop* your negative inner voice instantly.

In my experience the quicker a player stops negative thoughts the more effective this technique is. When a footballer allows an ANT to linger the more destructive it becomes. One ANT is quickly joined by other ANTs.

"This center back is playing really well. I can't find a way past him. Coach must think I'm rubbish."

Chapter 7

"If I don't start beating this center back I'm not going to score."

"I'm not sure I'm good enough to find a way through. He's just too strong and too quick. What's the point?"

"If I don't score my place in the team will be in doubt. I'll be gutted if I get dropped."

And so we have the infestation of ANTs that eat away at our performance. The more ANTs you have the more you fill your brain with the wrong kind of thinking. The brain slows down, you slow down. To be a great soccer player you can't afford to slow down physically and mentally.

Stopping ANTs is simple - just see a STOP sign in your mind. You see a big red STOP sign, the one you see on the side of a road. Or perhaps say STOP to yourself. You can scream it in your mind. *Stop*! You need something that you can consciously see or say that will snap you back into the present moment and instantly stop the ANTs from spreading.

Just as *spotting* requires practice and patience so does *stopping*. Once you feel comfortable spotting ANTs - start to stop them. Do this in training and in your everyday life. The more you practice the better you'll become at taking control of your ANTs.

Failure in football isn't fatal...
but thinking that it is... is!

SHIFT

So you've *spotted* the ANT and you've *stopped* the ANT - now you have to *shift* the ANT. You have to *shift* your negative thoughts to something more positive and something more constructive.

Once Carlton had become accustomed to spotting and stopping, I wanted him to take ownership of his inner voice as he played. I knew if he did he would play with the physicality that the size of his body suggested he could. He would also be able to utilize the skill and vision we all saw in him when he was in training mode.

I told Carlton that he needed two types of thinking on the pitch. He needed to think *confidently* and to think in a *helpful* way.

Every thought a player thinks, every action he takes determines the quality of his play every second of every game

Confident thinking

You're a soccer player, not a supporter. A fan is allowed to be negative. A fan is allowed to give up. A fan is allowed to voice disapproval. A fan is allowed to have ANTs. You are not!

You are a soccer player. You are a competitor. No-one and nothing should take you away from playing with 100% effort. You must have an abundance mentality. You must be an 'I can' player.

This was my message to Carlton. As he started to understand that he didn't need to be a slave to his self-talk, and that he could easily squash his ANTs, he began to realize an 'I can' mentality.

I'd like you to adopt the same mentality. I'd like you to squash your ANTs and shift to a more confident mindset. I'd like you to be an *'I can'* player. I want you to have the loud inner voice that started to resonate with Carlton – the mantra: *'stop, I can'*.

"Stop, I can score today."

"Stop, I can beat this full back. I can get the better of him."

"Stop, I can out jump this striker."

"Stop, we can win this today."

"Stop, I can keep this work rate up."

"Stop, forget the future, focus on the present."

Become an *'I can'* player. Become an expert at denying ANTs space in your PFC, retaining your visual awareness, anticipation and speed of decision making.

As an *'I can'* player you release a cocktail of brain chemicals that deliver peak performance – a chemical such as adrenaline which is useful because it drives your body toward your goals. Adrenaline sustains your effort for 90 minutes; it helps you compete hard in the last lung busting 10 minutes of a match. It enables a mind to maintain a tiring body.

An *'I can'* player is the definition of the oft used words *mentally tough*. Mental toughness is being dominant, strong and powerful when it's easy not to be. It's persisting when things are challenging – when everything around you says *stop*.

A striker must learn to be patient. She will miss more than she scores, but with patience on some days she will score more than she misses

Helpful thinking

Confident thinking may be enough for you. It will certainly help you play much more consistent football. It's enough to help carry you through challenging games. Use it and you will be a much tougher player. But you can do more. You can think in a way that goes beyond the vital *'I can'* mentality. You can learn to think in a *helpful* way.

It always excites me when one technique fuses into another. This is one of those times. To my mind thinking helpfully means returning your focus of attention back to your script. It means mentally going back to the plays you have chosen before the game.

Let me give you a few examples to bring helpful thinking alive. Let's imagine you are a central defender with a couple of plays in your script. These plays are *'to be constantly vocal'* and *'to stay tight to the striker when in the box.'* Your team has conceded a goal and it's the striker you are marking who's scored. You immediately get an ANT.

"I can't believe he got in behind me there, coach is gonna have a real go at me at half time. I don't think I can contain this guy he's so quick."

Now your job is simple – you have to squash this ANT, and quickly.

"Stop, I can contain this striker. Goals happen, I just have to get back to staying tight to him. Keep playing with confidence. Come on!"

Now that's one squashed ANT. You've encouraged yourself and you're helping yourself get through a bad patch, through a mistake. If you don't do this then you've got a real problem. You're going to let yourself down as an individual and as a team mate.

Let's test out another example. You're a winger and you've been instructed by your coach to get as many balls into the box as you can. So you have one major play in your script: *"ball into the box as quickly as possible"*. But the full back marking you is doing a good job. He's showing you on the inside, onto your weaker foot and it's difficult for you to whip a ball into the penalty area. Your ANT pops into your head.

"This full back is showing me inside every time. I can't get that ball in the box with any pace."

Solution time again. Squash that ANT.

"Stop, I can whip this ball into the area. If I'm on my weak foot - commit to it 100%. But also just keep trying to get down the line. I'll get plenty of crosses in."

Remember, this conversation (or argument) with yourself happens in a split second. The brain really does work that quickly. And your ANTs are squashed behind closed doors in the dark of your own mind. This isn't something that people see. It's in your own private world.

A player should commit to letting nothing bother him on the pitch. When he does this he can be immersed in the process of playing

Be proactive

Carlton Cole became an England international because he committed to the process of improvement. We worked hard together but he also learnt greatly from his managers Alan Curbishley and Gianfranco Zola. He spent time speaking with the coaching staff at West Ham, to great coaches such as Glynn Snodin and Steve Clarke.

Above all Carlton was enormously proactive with his inner voice on the pitch. He proactively used both confident and helpful thinking. He refused to allow ANTs to settle and destroy his performance mindset. He threw them away before they infested his PFC.

When he won his first cap for England he stood on the side of the pitch squashing ANTs as he readied himself to come on against the then European champions, Spain. He had every reason to be flooded with ANTs. He was playing his first game for his country, broadcast live on TV around the world and he was competing against the world's best football team. Instead he focused his mind on thinking in a confident and helpful manner. He focused on the plays in his script that he had set himself earlier in the week. The ones he had been picturing religiously leading up to the game.

When he ran onto the pitch as a second half substitute he did so with a clear, confident mind. He was ready to play with focus and freedom.

Relentless should the player be on match day. Relentlessly positive, relentlessly focused, relentlessly driven. That's a learnable skill

But he did have one more secret - a technique that when combined with a strong inner voice will pack an unparalleled peak performance punch. I'll reveal this secret in the next chapter as we continue to work on your soccer mindset.

8

Stokesy the Greyhound

Being supremely gifted at something doesn't automatically invite you to the table of champions. My work with young talented soccer players has shown me that the make-up of someone who competes at the highest level in any discipline takes more than just the possession of an abundance of talent. Getting to the top requires desire, focus, determination, grit and self-belief.

In fact a gift can be a curse. Finding something easy from the start can prevent you from developing key mindset skills that elite level careers so often hinge on. This is something my friend Anthony Stokes found out early in his career.

Stokesy's story

At 15 years old things looked bright for young Anthony Stokes. As a precocious 14 year old striker (the best Ireland had to offer in his age group) Arsenal FC had paid a seven figure fee to bring him to the famous London football academy. And now at 15 he had broken into the Arsenal reserve team. Talent, backed up by the strong work ethic his father had helped him develop as a young boy, had born fruit. But by the time I met him in December 2009 his career hadn't quite taken off as had been predicted.

At 21 Anthony left Arsenal for Sunderland FC but failed to make an impact and within 2 years was granted a free transfer to Scottish club Hibernian. And after scoring just 4 goals in one season Anthony asked to do a little work with me. I met him at a snowy Edinburgh airport and liked him immediately. Friendly, warm and down to earth he casually told me his thoughts about his game and his dreams for the future. We got to work straight away and it didn't take long to discover what he *really* needed to learn, develop and improve.

The intensity of sport

Every sport is different. If you are entering the Olympics as an archer being 'pumped up' like a wrestler probably won't lead to a gold medal winning performance. If on the other hand you are climbing into the ring as a boxer, your trainer will soon be picking you off the floor if you are as relaxed and calm as a competitor in a pistol shooting tournament.

Every sport requires a performance at a different level of intensity. Soccer is different to golf, just as baseball is different to rugby.

My definition of intensity of performance relates to both the physical and mental components of the game. To me intensity is your physical activity and mental alertness. Essentially the mental side is a form of focus - how mentally lively you are during performance. In the language of football it's being 'up for it'. The physical side relates to how much ground you cover and how you use your body. So, in football terms, your work rate, energy, and strength on and off the ball.

Soccer is a physical game. It's a game of speed, strength, stamina and power. A soccer player must be alert, alive, lively and aware – switched on at all times. He must work hard, keep up with play and complete a succession of sprints to close the opposition down or win the ball. He must be strong in a challenge on the ground and in the air. He must be loud with his vocals and show a commanding presence as he competes. Intensity in soccer must be high enough to deliver this show of physicality. However, the footballer must also be intelligent. He must be a problem solver knowing what plays to make and knowing how to deal effectively with the opposition. He must execute tactics that have been set before the game by his coach. He must have fire in his belly but he must also have ice in his mind. There must be thought behind the movement and the runs he makes and there must be a plan. So a soccer player's performance intensity can't be so high that he simply runs around like a headless chicken.

You can't force 'the zone'. But you can tick the
boxes that make it more likely

Everyone is different: intensity scales

Walking through the changing room of a football team, with the hustle and bustle
of players getting ready to play, you couldn't help but notice that few
commonalities exist between the players in terms of who they are as people.
Everyone is a little different to each other. Each player has a different personality
combined with different experiences, backgrounds, expectations, fears, hopes,
desires, beliefs, wants, temperaments and values.

Some are loud while others are quiet. Some wear their heart on their sleeve while
others remain passive in the corner. Some like to dance before they play while
others like to sit and think. Some are from a rich upbringing, some only know the
trappings of poverty. Some are friendly, some are aloof. Some have great dreams,
others are content. Some are artists, some are warriors – some are a little of both.
This rich tapestry of individuality shapes the nature of the game. It drives the
different styles in which the game can be played.

So intensity cannot be set at one fixed point. But if we were to imagine a scale
from 1 through to 10 with lower numbers representing a more relaxed
performance intensity, and higher numbers related to greater performance
intensity, then to my mind 6 would be an average of the ideal intensity of mindset
and physicality. Most players would fit somewhere in between 5 and 7.

Watch a Carlos Tevez play and you see 7 out of 10. He is very lively with an
exceptional work rate. Tevez is a warrior! Slightly lower would be Paul Scholes
at about 6 out of 10. Lower still at about 5 out of 10 would be an Eric Cantona or
a Dimitar Berbatov. These players are usually artists – highly skilled players who
compete at the top level due to their vision and subtle touch rather than their
energy and fire.

What is your correct level of intensity when performing?

*Fight in soccer is measured by intensity, strength
& a never say die focus. A player who fights every
second of every game never loses*

The correct mental and physical intensity

Get the right *mental intensity* and you'll have the added benefits of sharpened focus, heightened awareness and the feeling of being in 'the zone'. This can have great knock on effects for your *physical intensity*. You can play with added power, speed, stamina and energy. However, too much mental intensity and you will play with a distracted mindset or tunnel vision focus. As a headless chicken you won't see, or be aware of, what is going on around you - only what is in front of you. You'll make errors in decision making and you'll potentially play with too much speed and power.

The correct physical intensity is not only set by your mental intensity but also by the tactics your team employs. Your coach may wish you to relax on the ball and play the simple pass rather than play a kick-and-rush style of game. He may want you to stand off the opposition rather than hurriedly press them. This type of game is more in line with a physical intensity level of 5.

You can still play at a *mental intensity* of 6 even if your *physical intensity* has to drop due to tactics or style of play. An example of this is the style of play from the best team in the world right now – Barcelona. When they lose the ball the man closest to the opposition in possession will increase intensity to 7 by pressing hard. If he hasn't won the ball within 5 seconds he'll relax and drop his intensity to 6. When they regain possession, to begin with they'll drop to an intensity of 5 as they pass the ball around and then pick up to 6 as they probe for gaps and move into empty spaces as quickly as possible to receive the ball.

To express your physicality on the pitch you have to play with the correct mental and physical intensity, and you must maintain this as best you can for 90 minutes. And that's an enormous challenge. It isn't easy to accomplish. Sure there are times you can really relax (when a player is injured or during an enforced break in play) but, by and large, you need to stick around the 6 region on our scale of 1 to 10.

Again, have a little think about your ideal performance intensity.

I'm unsure where the body ends & the mind begins. But I know a footballer needs to work on both if he is immersed in excellence

Intensity: the nature of the game

Whilst it is vitally important to play at the right intensity it isn't easy either to find the correct level, or maintain it. The game throws up so many situations that can lessen or increase your intensity. Let me give you a couple of examples of intensity destroyers:

- Making a mistake
- Going a goal down
- Intimidation from the opposition
- Great play from the opposition
- The crowd
- Feedback from your coach
- Feedback from your team mates

If something goes wrong on the pitch, such as you make a mistake, then your levels can drop from 6 to 4 because intensity works hand in hand with ANTs. Confidence and intensity so often take a dive together. Similarly a rush of blood to the head due to a foul can increase intensity from 6 to 8 and liberate your anger. Emotion is a subject we will explore in the next chapter but briefly increased intensity associated with anger often delivers poor technique, red cards and conceded goals.

The power to play hard to the end, to play honestly to the end, to play with passion to the end...comes from within

Intensity: as you are

My diagnosis of Anthony Stokes targeted his intensity of performance. To my mind he didn't play with enough mental or physical intensity. He was too much the artist and not enough of a warrior. He was too relaxed as he played and his work rate was low. I explained to him that he had to learn how to get himself 'psyched up for the match' and learn how to stay at the right intensity for the whole game.

On the pitch he had great vision, awareness and speed of thought and could weight a pass perfectly. However, at times during the game, he displayed a serious lack of intensity. I strongly believed he could become a better team mate as well as score more goals with a greater feeling of intensity. He had to become more of a warrior. But he had to do this without sacrificing the artist within him.

Now please don't misunderstand me, his lack of intensity wasn't because he didn't want to work hard for himself and for the team. Anthony Stokes was and is a passionate young man who wants to win and score goals for himself and his team. However, he's naturally a laid back guy and he had been a little guilty of taking that side of his personality out onto the pitch with him. No-one had ever taught him how to have a 'game face'.

I'm pretty sure I was the first person in his professional life to explain to him the intensity challenges that lay before him. Just like every other component in soccer, performance intensity is a skill and I explained to Anthony that this *skill* could be learnt - he could change things. So we got to work and set about improving his intensity so he could work harder for the team, defend from the front better, get into better positions and become a more consistent goal scorer. .

Great soccer players have a hand on the gear stick. They can move up & down their intensity levels effortlessly when appropriate

Intensity: know yourself, know your game

Let me ask you five questions that will help you learn a little about your ideal level of performance intensity.

- Are you an artist or a warrior?
- Are you a laid back individual or do you possess a more passionate, fiery personality?
- What level of intensity have you displayed in the past that's worked for you?
- What position do you play?
- How does your coach like your team to play?

These questions give you important clues into the mental and physical intensity you should be playing at in your team.

A soccer player cannot will victory. But he can will effort, focus & freedom. It is strength of mind that pulls a player through 90 minutes

Getting up: Using your body

This may be a book about the mind but your body plays a vital role in managing how you think and feel. As I say to clients – as much as your psychology affects your physiology, so your physiology affects your psychology. I strongly believe that some of the most powerful techniques in psychology are the ones that involve deliberately changing behavior, action and movement to think and feel differently. Let me introduce you to one such idea, a technique Carlton Cole consistently used to maintain his performance intensity as he competed.

A footballer should be a great actor. If you are down then act confidently. If you lose focus then act focused. Physiology changes psychology

Chapter 8

Head and shoulders

The technique *head and shoulders* came about because a lot of my working life has been spent preaching the benefits of body language. It sounds obvious doesn't it, the idea of keeping great body language as you play. But it's not always easy to use your body language to manage your mind.

As a soccer player I want to see you play with dynamic body language. I want you to stand confidently. I want to see you on your toes at all times with a sense of alertness and readiness. I want you to be explosive with your footwork, loud in your communication, aggressive in the challenge, and strong in the air.

Scientists are starting to understand more and more that your body affects how you think and feel. By adjusting and changing your body language you can change your feelings of performance intensity – you can change your mental alertness and physical activity.

When your feelings of performance intensity decrease all you have to do is get your body moving. This will release the kind of chemicals into your brain and body that help you feel the correct intensity again. These kinds of chemicals include adrenaline, noradrenaline and dopamine. These are chemicals that sustain your effort, that keep you alert, that supercharge your body for action.

Here is a very simple technique to get your body moving at times of low intensity. In Britain there is a song that all school kids sing called "head, shoulders, knees and toes". I think this song is sung by children the world over. I want you to think of the term head, shoulders, knees and toes as you play. Let's break this down:

- Head – Head up, eyes open, communicate
- Shoulders – stand tall, use hand and arm gestures
- Knees and toes – get on your toes and move; avoid being static

I love this image of head, shoulders, knees, toes. It's a great picture to have when it comes to building and maintaining the correct performance intensity. I want to see your head up at all times, looking around and being vocal with team mates. I want to see you stand tall with your shoulders up. And I want to see you on your toes, willing to run and feeling on the move at all times.

Give the ball away – head, shoulders, knees, toes

Go a goal down – head, shoulders, knees, toes

Constantly lose an aerial battle – head, shoulders, knees, toes

I want you to be head, shoulders, knees and toes for 90 minutes. Take some time to visualize this:

What do you look like with head, shoulders, knees, toes? What do you look like when you're always looking around with loud vocals, shoulders up, always on your toes. Always on the move?

Feeling the heat on the pitch? Reduce the temperature by playing on your toes, by turning up the volume of your vocals & move, move, move

Carlton Cole versus Spain (England debut)

Let nothing and no-one take you out of your perfect performance intensity. You will squash ANTs and you will maintain head, shoulders, knees and toes every minute you play in this match. You will keep your head up looking for spaces and looking for opportunities to threaten the Spanish defense. You will stand tall – you will ONLY stand tall. This will help you lessen the confidence of your opposition. It will help you use all of your height and all of your power. Let nothing and no-one take you out of your perfect performance intensity. You will stay alert, alive and ready. You will be on your toes at all times ready to receive the ball, ready to punish the opposition. You will be head, shoulders, knees and toes every second you compete...

This was my message to Carlton. And he executed it perfectly when he came on in the 75th minute to make his debut against the best team in the world. He was alert, alive and lively. He delivered a performance full of intensity and went close to scoring a few times.

Chapter 8

*Movement is at the heart of a footballer's game.
With this in mind he must keep his body language
alert and ready at all times*

The animal technique

This is the process I took Anthony through. Have a go yourself.

I asked Anthony what it would look like if he performed with more intensity on the pitch in a match.

I would be constantly on my toes and on the move. I would come deep to collect the ball and would go out wide to make a challenge. I would press defenders and try to get the ball back if I lost it. I would be a constant pain for the defenders. I would be sharp in my movement to make space and to receive the ball. I would be constantly looking for space.

Once he had a clear picture of this I asked him what might be thought of as quite a strange question. *"If you were an animal playing like this - what animal would you be?"* I helped put my question into perspective by telling him that it probably wouldn't be a tortoise as tortoises are slow and lethargic creatures. I asked him what animal he pictured when he thought of the kind of work rate and intensity he was envisioning.

Admittedly he had a bit of a laugh at my question but after thinking about it for a minute or so he came up with a *'greyhound'*. I pressed him further.

A greyhound reminds me of running fast, being alert and sharp, always on the move, being keen, eager and hungry to run. Nipping on people's heels... a greyhound can be a real nuisance.

Right away we both loved the image of a greyhound on the pitch. So Anthony Stokes decided to play soccer like a greyhound.

He went to work at this right away in training. Every single training session he strove to be a *greyhound* on the pitch. He held an image of playing 'like a greyhound' every single day in every single training session. Straight away this technique shifted his body language, changed the pictures in his head, and altered the emotions he felt on the pitch.

Rather than being too laid back and relaxed he started to feel more upbeat and determined. He started to feel 'up for it'. The pictures he had in his mind were images of hard work and non-stop running. His body language portrayed that of a winner: upbeat, alert, and ready for battle.

If you need to play with greater intensity why not try the same technique. What do you look like in your role on the pitch when you play at the right intensity level? What is your movement like? What is your work ethic like? What about your body language? What are you like in the air? What about in the tackle? What is your communication like? What words best describe your actions? A few might be: dominant, strong, powerful, committed.

Okay, now with a clear image in your mind of your perfect performance intensity level have a go at answering this question. If an animal was playing instead of you, playing your dream game, what would that animal be? What animal would have similar playing characteristics?

Your animal might be:

➤ Cheetah
➤ Gorilla
➤ Lion
➤ Greyhound
➤ Rottweiler
➤ Tiger

It sounds a little strange doesn't it, but associating a performance to an animal can make a difference to your game. Why? Well for me the main reason is because animals are superior to humans physically. When you associate your game to say a greyhound you will get pictures in your mind of running at super human speed, getting around the pitch, and generally being a very hard working soccer player. It's a perfect image for you to have.

Stokesy took his animal with him onto the pitch on match day. He even wrote the word 'greyhound' on his hand to remind him as he played. Whenever he *spotted* himself losing intensity he reminded himself by saying *"greyhound, greyhound. Be greyhound"* in his mind. This reminder re-energized him, lifted his body language and got him on his toes ready to move, and ready to lose his markers and receive the ball.

So by all means if you have an animal in mind write it on your hand before you play. Your 'animal' is a perfect cue word to keep you playing at intensity.

*Mind affects body, body affects mind. Being on
your toes wakens the mind*

The 12 second greyhound

Only a month or so into our working relationship Anthony produced a moment of pure Greyhound. Our objective had been to allow the first 10 minutes to set the intensity of the game. I wanted Anthony to get off to an explosive start – to be as busy and as energetic as he could be. I wanted him to be a greyhound from the off. Just before New Year 2010 the Greyhound lined up for Hibernian against Rangers.

The Greyhound kicked off and raced forward to offer himself in an advanced position straight away. The ball was played to Moroccan midfielder Merouane Zemmama who skillfully weaved his way past a Rangers midfielder and took it deep into the Rangers' half. Ahead of him the Greyhound had sprinted into the penalty box. He lost his marker with quick acceleration and to the far right edge of the area he opened his body to receive the ball. Zemmama spotted him and played a simple pass to the Greyhound's feet. The Greyhound was in space but had a tight angle to shoot from. He struck the ball perfectly. It ricocheted off the post and into the net. Just 12.4 seconds into the game the Greyhound had scored. The fastest goal in Scottish Premier League history.

Ways to slow you down

Let's now examine the problem of playing with too much intensity. If a lazy looking player is unattractive and ineffective then someone who runs around like a headless chicken on the pitch can be just as destructive to himself and to his team mates. Psychologists use the term 'over-arousal' for this. A player can be too highly charged for a match. He can get too involved and subsequently may not maintain his shape or position. He may make reckless challenges. Too much performance intensity shuts down game intelligence. Awareness becomes tunneled and ball skills become uncoordinated. A footballer with an intensity of 8, 9, or 10 will become ineffective and may get himself sent off.

There are several effective ways to deal with performance intensity that is too high. Let's examine a few.

Breathe

Breathing is a great way to help you slow down on the pitch and relax. This is because it takes very little thought to engage. You're not thinking of a complex strategy (using up crucial brain juice) you are simply taking some deep breaths.

These breaths engage the part of the nervous system that slows you down and de-stresses you. It enables you to take control of mind and body in a matter of seconds – quicker than any other technique.

Simply by spotting your high performance intensity and briefly shifting your attention to your breathing is enough to slow you. The spikes of adrenaline that have taken over your body will lessen and you will be able to think with clarity in no time.

Slowly does it

Quite often awareness of your performance intensity will come from an outside person. A team mate or a coach might tell you to relax or calm down. And to be honest 'relax' is what you need to do. How can you do this other than taking some breaths? Simple! Slow everything down. Slow down your movements, slow down your actions. Take a little more time on the ball, stay disciplined by keeping your position.

Say the words "*relax*" and "*calm*" to yourself. Remind yourself why it's important not to rush around on the pitch.

Chapter 8

Soccer is a game of intelligence as much as it's a physical game. It's a game of out-thinking your opponent. You need your PFC switched on at all times, not over-loaded so it turns itself off.

It must again be emphasized that your physiology affects your psychology. You can use your physicality to lessen your intensity. Stop diving in, hold your shape. Stop distributing the ball so quickly, hold on to it, get your head up and wait. You probably have more time than you think. And to be effective you need this time. A striker may have delayed his run by a split second. Waiting a little before making your pass can lead to a goal.

Soccer is a game of intelligence so give yourself the best chance to use your brain. Give yourself the ability in the moment to execute the tactics the coach has laid down. Manage yourself by managing your body, your direction of attention, your breathing, and your self-talk. These are simple ideas but not always easy to deliver. Especially when overwhelming emotion creeps into our mindset.

9

Why Birch Stayed Down

26th May 2003. English League 2 Play Off Final.
Winners get promoted. Losers get nothing.

A player in the middle of the park delights his club's supporters with a shock of blue and white hair – his team's colors. He weaves in and out of the opposition, makes strong challenges, plays crisp passes to team mates and gets shots away when he can. He's all over the field – full of passion, desire and want.

The game is end to end. Full of the excitement any final produces. The player with the blue and white hair receives the ball on the half way but then goes down after a strong challenge. He's left crumpled in a heap, the tackle a foul - deliberate and unfair. A wave of anger surges through his body. The red mist starts to descend. But this time he's going to win. This time he's not going to let anger overrule his heart and mind. This time he's going to stay down.

Marc Bircham's Mindset

Born a QPR fan, will die a QPR fan. That's Marc Bircham.

The only soccer player on the planet never to have set foot in the country he represented at international level, Marc Bircham (or Birch for short) was born in London but played internationally for Canada. When he competed for his club,

QPR, he sported blue and white hair to complement the color of the team's kit. Similarly when he set foot on the pitch for Canada he dyed a red and white streak into his hair to demonstrate his loyalties to his national team.

Always passionate, Birch would admit that he was never the most naturally gifted young soccer player. But it was his determination, grit, and sheer force of will that helped him carve out a successful career as a footballer in the lower leagues in England. And playing in the second and third tier of English football suited him. Physically more competitive than the Premier League this level of soccer demands work rate, strength, guts and drive. Skill finishes a distant second behind physicality.

But sometimes Birch was a little too combative. In fact all too often he crossed the murky line between competitiveness and aggression. He would fly in with heavy challenges and allow the tackles from opposition players to wind him up.

Competing, anger and aggression

I have travelled far and wide giving presentations to soccer teams and what always fascinates me most is the response to the question I often ask: "Who here plays their best soccer when angry?"

I would say about 80% of the room raises their hand. Surprised? I was - at first.

What I soon learnt was that the anger a player can feel following an altercation with an opponent, or perhaps from a disagreement with the referee, changes performance intensity levels. When it ups gears to 7 out of 10 on the intensity scale the player may experience benefits to his game. He may be able to play with greater strength, sharpness and speed. This is a product of the link between mind and body. During moments of anger a footballer can unlock his body's evolutionary potential to compete with all of its physicality.

But let's be clear. If anger pushes your performance intensity a little above the norm then your play can improve. But if it breaks through the 8 or 9 barriers then the headless chicken will emerge.

Let's pause to think about two players who have been known to have 'anger management issues' on the pitch: Roy Keane and Wayne Rooney in the English Premier League.

For both of these players anger is their best friend and their worst enemy. How is it their best friend? Just as I've described. Their anger helps increase their feelings of physical intensity and mental alertness. In their state of anger they can be quicker to the ball, more competitive in their challenges, stronger in the air, and they can anticipate with speed. Their anger can sustain their effort, magnify their focus, and deliver surges of adrenaline that improves performance all around.

However this injection of performance intensity is only useful for them if they direct it toward executing their role and responsibility. It's only helpful if the intensity of anger is directed toward being more *competitive*. It is when they direct their anger intensity toward aggressiveness that things can go wrong.

The most important battle the soccer player faces on the pitch is with herself

Reactive and proactive

To my mind when a soccer player feels angry he is more likely to be reactive. A reactive mindset is one where aggression takes over and the player commits fouls, argues with the referee and opposition (and sometimes team mates) and plays with a lack of intelligence and at too high a tempo. Wayne Rooney and Roy Keane, no matter how great they have been as players have been guilty of doing just that – directing their feelings of anger toward being aggressive on the pitch. This has rendered them ineffective at times and gotten them sent off. When they are *reactive* they aren't world class. They aren't the best team player and they hurt and punish themselves rather than their opponents.

People often excuse players for being reactive. "*They want to win*" is often their explanation. Well if they want to win so badly they need to learn to manage their mindset, use their anger intensity wisely, and stay on the pitch (rather than being sent off). They need to play intelligently. They need to be *proactive* with their response.

I understand that human emotion is a very complex phenomenon and I understand that in the *heat of the moment* people do rash things. I *get* that footballers want to compete hard and I appreciate the need to unsettle the opposition with physicality. But proactive responses, no matter the pressure, no matter the situation, can be learnt - responses that are best for you as a player and best for your team mates.

I would be the last person who would want to extinguish the fire that burns bright in my clients. But I want them, just as I want you, to value intelligent, proactive soccer. I want them and you to understand that you can't win when you're in headless chicken mode or if you've been sent off. It really is that simple. I'd like you to carry that philosophy onto the pitch with you.

The art of mental toughness is making the uncomfortable as comfortable as is possible

The English Premier League

Full of passion and non-stop action. I feel blessed to work with players, and in organizations, that regularly compete in the best football league in the world. But because of the style of play - I regularly turn on my TV to see players guilty of drawing on their anger in the wrong way.

I remember watching a Premier League match a couple of years ago between Wigan Athletic and Arsenal. Wigan were very much the underdogs but after 80 minutes they found themselves winning one nil and in the 81st minute they had a definite penalty turned down by the referee. Collectively they went mad. They were seething at the referee and quite a few of the players went to argue with the match officials.

Up until that moment they had been playing great. They had been matching a skillful Arsenal team for passing. They had been full of energy. But the incident disrupted their focus. They became more interested in remonstrating with the referee than focusing on their tasks – their roles and responsibilities. They were busy feeling sorry for themselves. They lost their discipline and shape. Individually their game intelligence disappeared. They were unable to read and predict the pattern of play.

After the controversial incident Arsenal went straight on the attack and within a minute, with the entire Wigan defense at sea, Arsenal equalized. An angry Wigan team were now really seething with rage. They felt they should have had a penalty and a chance to make it two nil, but now it was one all. And I don't think I need to tell you what happened next. Within 5 minutes Arsenal scored to go 2-1 up and went on to win the game. To say controversy surrounded the last 10 minutes is an understatement but let's examine those last few minutes a little closer.

The Wigan players were very angry, furious even, at the decisions that had been made. Collectively they had a surge in intensity but instead of this energizing and helping them - they directed their intensity toward the match officials. They chose to direct that intensity toward arguing about what they deemed to be unfair.

If, however, they had directed that intensity toward their roles and responsibilities they would have maybe started playing even better than they had played in the previous 80 minutes. They could have used that intensity to build on their lead, work like crazy, and defend with strength and aggression. They would have given themselves the best opportunity to win.

Far better to exact revenge on a fouling opponent
by placing energy & resources onto executing
your skills than onto the opponent

Directing your anger: the proactive mindset

Is directing your anger easy to do? Of course not! But it is *essential* if you want to be the best you can be. In a proactive mindset you use anger in the right way. You *use* your body, your breathing, or your self-talk, proactively to deal with your feelings of anger in the moment, all of which helps you direct your anger correctly. There are several things you can do when the red mist starts to descend.

Chapter 9

Birch's trick: using body and mind

After receiving a series of red cards Marc Bircham decided he had to change things. He learnt that whilst he couldn't necessarily change or control the sudden rush of anger he felt when he thought something unfair had happened he realized he could control how he reacted and responded to the situation. He could be proactive.

It was often after a strong challenge that he started to feel anger. He would immediately think about getting up and starting a fight with the player who'd tackled him. Or he'd instantly decide he was going to get the player back at some stage during the game (a reaction that would lead to him being sent off).

To deal with these reactive thoughts Birch decided that when he got tackled he'd spend another few seconds on the ground. Instead of getting up immediately to seek retribution he would lay a little longer on the pitch. These vital few seconds enabled him to collect his thoughts. It allowed him to remind himself that the best way to get one up on the opposition wasn't to physically fight anyone, but to channel his feelings of energy into his game.

"That tackle could have broken my leg. I'm mad... STOP... ok, good, lets channel this into my game. Stay focused... be first to the ball. Punish them with a goal."

It sounds basic (and perhaps contrived) when written down but the combination of staying down a little longer and rationalizing the situation enabled Birch to deal more effectively with his anger. He started to use his extra feelings of intensity in the right way. He became a proactive intelligent player.

Football is like life. Success comes to the one who manages himself best

Whatever feels comfortable

You feel anger? Then take some deep breaths to talk to yourself in a calm rational way. Or maybe do what Birch does and use your body - stay down, or walk away, or go and speak to a team mate. Just do something different.

"STOP... I'm feeling angry and I feel energized but I have to use this energy in the right way. Remember my script... "First to the ball" and "box to box." Let's get those right."

Being proactive with your mindset, with your inner voice, is a choice. You can choose to spot that you're feeling angry and you can choose to stop that destructive inner voice that will push you to seek retribution and foul a bunch of players. You can choose to shift your focus onto the plays in your script. You can choose to use the greater feelings of intensity you experience because of anger and execute your script with passion. That is competitiveness and that is the mark of a champion. It is a sign of maturity and an indication that you are in complete control of your mindset.

A champion copes with whatever the opposition throws at him by staying focused on his script. If you're aggressive you are not focused on your plays - your attention has been caught up in the opposition, the referee or something else you can't control.

If you get tackled hard and feel angry use the anger toward your script. If you miss a few chances and start to feel angry use the energy toward your script. If a team mate has a go at you and you start to boil over use your angry energy toward your script.

If you're reading this and you admit to letting anger get the better of you on the pitch take some time to picture what that anger looks like. I bet you feel a little stupid when you actually step back and think about the aggressiveness you portray when you play. Shouting at team mates, hacking at the legs of the opposition, balling at the referee. Does that help you to play great? Does that help your team to win?

If that's you then take a little time to change that picture. Watch an inner movie of yourself playing in a competitive manner. You get fouled and you get back up, focus, and play hard. The referee makes a strange decision which you ignore and you mark-up. Does that type of proactive mindset guarantee excellence or ensure victory every time? Of course not! But it gives you a better chance.

Chapter 9

Be patient. Accept! The game brings with it some crazy moments. Just keep your head by using the feelings of intensity you experience when angry in an intelligent, proactive manner, and you will surprise yourself.

10

Kevin's 10,000 hours

It wasn't a gift from birth that helped him score 62 goals as a youth team player in a single season. It was Acton Park, or more precisely the thousands of hours he spent there with his two brothers practicing and playing football.

The park in Acton is just a stone's throw away from Loftus Road, the home of QPR FC and whenever Kevin Gallen went out to play with his brothers Steve and Joe he could see the top of the stadium's floodlights glistening in the sun. His motivation was visible at all times!

Kevin went on to have a successful career as a Premiership striker, a career largely as a result of the amount he practiced and the manner in which he trained. Recent science is showing us that the way we practice determines how good we become at something. This chapter explores the art and science of training and how to develop the soccer game of your dreams.

10,000 hours

There is one figure that lays on the lips of many of the world's finest sports coaches right now – 10,000. It is this number that is believed to be one of the secrets to success.

Practice soccer for 10,000 hours and you give yourself a great chance of becoming world class at what you do. But not all soccer fans should get too excited yet. There are, of course, rules and regulations to those 10,000 hours. Some of which I'll talk about later.

It was a Swedish researcher called Anders Ericsson who came up with the magic number. He discovered that experts practice around the same amount of time every single day including at weekends.

Back in the 1980s Ericsson travelled to Berlin to study the working patterns of top violinists. At the time, people thought that the really top violinists would train for fewer hours than the less accomplished musicians because they had natural talent and 'didn't need to practice'. But Ericsson discovered the complete opposite. The best violinists were the ones who invested significantly more time to practice. As a result, over the past 20 years, Anders Ericsson has argued that people can, by and large, reach excellence in their chosen profession or activity but it takes about 10,000 hours of hard work to do so.

He says this:

"With the exception of the influence of height and body size in some sports, no characteristic of the brain or body has yet been shown to constrain an individual from reaching an expert level."

And Ericsson discovered more interesting facts. He found that the great violinists tended to take a nap or rest after lunch. The violinists told him that the only way they could keep full concentration was to take regular breaks and limit the amount of hours they practiced per day. They said they felt that without a fully focused mindset they were wasting their time.

Anders Ericsson argues that not only do the world's best become the best because they practice more - but they reach excellence because they practice with greater focus and intensity.

Deliberate practice

Let's get in our imaginary time machine and head back over 20 years.

Kevin's twelve year old brain is overloaded. The ball is popped between Steve and Joe with ease and Kevin's task is to win it back from them. He knows he has to read their body shape – he has to pinpoint subtle body movements that tell him whether they will pass or feign and try to go around him. As Joe comes at him Kevin opens up his body so he can check his left shoulder to get a good look at Steve's movement. Timing the tackle is everything and as he sees Joe work another step over, Kevin intuitively knows Joe will try and go around him. As Joe side-foots the ball to the right Kevin sticks his foot out and knocks the ball away from Joe, away from danger. Kevin is learning the art of defense. He is learning how to shape his body, how to see others, and how to time a tackle.

Every day at the park Kevin's brain was overwhelmed by a whirlwind of information. When Steve and Joe invited their older mates to come play, Kevin was the youngest and smallest and had to think quickly to deal with the bigger players' physicality. He learnt to lose his marker by using his weight and body shape - he pretended to go one way then quickly shifted in another direction. He became adept at finding space by looking up more than everyone else. He learnt to go around defenders not by pace but by throwing a shape. Body angle left, move right. And he learnt to score goals, lots of them, by using his movement to get in front of defenders and by taking first time shots without care of outcome.

Kevin's education as a football player was the exact mode of practice that Anders Ericsson calls deliberate practice.

Deliberate practice isn't easy and it begins in the brain. It's not a soccer player doing an hour of training, doing a bit of five-a-side and having fun with mates. It's mentally and physically taxing. It is a kind of focused, repetitive practice in which you are always monitoring your performance, correcting, experimenting, listening to immediate and constant feedback, and always pushing beyond what you have already achieved.

Let's examine the attributes of deliberate practice in relation to the way Kevin developed his football.

 A footballer has to amaze himself everyday with his effective thinking, focus of attention & goal driven training

Chapter 10

Repetition: Kevin practiced a lot!

Deliberate practice centers on repetition. Champions become champions because they practice over and over again, no matter what the weather, no matter what the conditions. Don't expect to become any good at anything without doing it a lot!

Some of the greatest soccer players of all time come from a background of poverty. Pele grew up in Sao Paulo in Brazil, so poor that he couldn't afford a soccer ball and was often forced to play with a sock tied to a piece of string or with a grapefruit. Maradona too was born into poverty and lived his first years in Villa Fiorito, a shantytown on the southern outskirts of Buenos Aires in Argentina. Both of these legends of the game practiced and practiced. They did so in dirt and mud. They did so despite not having the money for flash boots and state of the art soccer balls.

Just as the greatest swimmers swim hundreds of lengths every day and the greatest golfers hit thousands of golf balls every week - a footballer must dedicate himself to play and practice. Kevin Gallen describes Acton Park as his home from home. In school holidays he woke at dawn, put on his tracksuit and walked the couple of hundred meters to the park.

He took hundreds of thousands of touches on the ball, took thousands of shots and spent endless hours passing and tackling. He perfected his spot kicks over time by taking penalty after penalty against his older brothers who acted as keeper. At first they saved most of his shots and they made fun of his weak strikes. But over time the taunting grew quieter as the power in his legs and in his kicks grew greater and greater. He would score more times than they could even get a touch on the ball.

Like most youngsters Kevin and his brothers had a love for football you can almost touch. They had a compulsion to *play* just as much as a will to win. It was only darkness that ceased the repetitive practice and forced them inside.

A soccer player must play soccer, and work
at his soccer. It must be fun, but it
must also be constructive

Stretching: Kevin played against older, better players

Kevin was constantly challenged by those he played with every day. As a small 10 year old he played with his equally football obsessed brothers: Joe, who is now assistant manager at Millwall FC and 4 years older than Kevin, and Stephen, who is now Head of Academy at QPR, and 2 years older.

Because he was frequently playing with players who were bigger, stronger and quicker than him Kevin was always stretched as he competed. At a minimum he had to keep up with them, but his passion and approach was to find ways to beat them. This self-induced pressure forced him to focus his mind with a level of intensity that would be unusual for a teenage soccer player. It was this degree of focus that played a huge part in his rapid progress.

With a will to beat his brothers at football Kevin was required to build his skill levels quickly. This meant he couldn't allow himself to slouch or take a break for a few seconds. To his younger mind his brothers moved with speed and agility. He had no time to think about the past. Mistakes had to dissolve into the background so he could fix his focus on the present moment.

His will to improve extended to post training analysis. In his bedroom after dinner he reviewed and analyzed how well he did against them and asked himself how he could do even better the next day. He didn't write anything down but he kept a mental note of the components he had to work on.

Many hours of focused, goal directed training is your launch pad for improvement. Every minute of practice offers a learning experience. Striving to be a little better each day provides mental fuel on your journey to discovering how good you can be.

Feedback: His brothers told him 'like it was'

Kevin was always getting barracked by his brothers. They were always mickey taking when shots were struck poorly or passes went seriously astray. But underneath the 'banter' (as we call it in England) there were always instructional comments for Kevin. "*You shot when you should have passed there*" or "*You didn't get your head up... I was calling for it*" were the types of feedback Kevin grew accustomed to.

Kevin came away from the park every day with his head buzzing with ideas. Not only did he take time to self-analyze but he pondered the comments his brothers had made during the day's practice. If they had shouted at him for shooting he asked himself why he had shot and why the option to pass was better. If they'd moaned at him for missing the target he thought a little about how he could get better at hitting the target. If they'd barked at him for losing control of the ball he imagined ways to improve his first touch. Kevin reflected on his day of practice not as if it was just a game (although he had a lot of fun playing) but as if it was his obsession to improve – to get slightly closer to the performances of his older brothers.

Deliberate practice involves feedback - verbally from others, visually from watching yourself play, or kinesthetically (from your bodily feelings) from your own mind.

Most of the time you need feedback from an outside source, from a coach or mentor. Make sure this feedback is as specific as possible and is solution focused. You need a coach to tell you about your game, the things you can control. Ask your coach what he felt you did well, then ask him to tell you what he feels needs to go better. *"You need to win more headers"* is not specific enough. *"You need to time your jumps better to win more headers"* is more precise feedback and gives you something tangible to work on. Allow me to give you a few more examples of good and bad feedback.

"You need to stop letting goals in. You are good enough not to." vs. "Commit to catching the balls on crosses. Be confident in yourself and you'll jump higher than the opposition strikers. You're good enough to keep a clean sheet."

"Stop giving the ball away." vs. "Relax on your passes. Spot your man and commit confidently to your pass. Try to focus on getting a great strike on the ball and trust your body to kick it in the right direction."

"You are always fouling. Stop fouling." vs. "Stand the player up. Remain on your feet and stay focused as he tries to go around you."

Of course you can't control the initial feedback from your coach but you can ask him to elaborate. You can ask him to tell you exactly how he wants you to improve the *specific* area of the game he gives you feedback on.

Remember, a great coach is only as good as his students are at learning. So take ownership of your feedback and communicate with your coach. Keep asking him what specifically you have to do to improve your game.

Working hard is important,
working correctly is crucial

How you should train

Train a little more

How often do you practice and train? Very few people reading this book are professional soccer players. Very few people can (or want) to make a living from the game. But if you are a recreational player who enjoys playing on a weekend for your local team or playing five-a-side with work colleagues then please do take a little more time to practice your game.

You'll be amazed how much you can improve just by turning up to the pitch 30 minutes earlier than normal to do a little more practice. Take a few shots, put some cones out and dribble around them. Invite a friend so he can go in goal or so he can try to tackle you in a one-versus-one.

If you train twice a week then an extra hour over those 2 sessions turns into 4 hours over the course of a month. So you will put in another 40-50 hours a year for just an extra small effort 2 days a week.

See a little more

Improvement starts in the brain so it's important you make your practice and training as mentally demanding as possible. It's easiest to do this in your extra practice. Make your shooting practice tougher by making the goal smaller. Place 2 bibs inside the goal, a couple of meters apart, and try to hit between the bibs from different angles. Maybe get a team mate to put you under pressure by closing you down quickly. If you are dribbling around cones then put those cones at ever decreasing distances apart so your ball control has to get better and better.

There are a whole set of drills you can do on your own or with a partner. The main message from the concept of deliberate practice is that soccer drills have to make you stretch your mind. They must be mentally demanding and physically

131

challenging. They must make you think and they must pinpoint your focus.

In football most of your sessions are set by the coach so it is up to you how you make the sessions mentally tougher for yourself. You could try to complete a passing drill with your head up more - checking your shoulders before the ball arrives at your feet. With drills that require a good first touch you could stretch yourself by trying to constantly improve your ability to deaden the speed of the ball. Similarly, if a drill involves running then you could strive to execute the drill while working on your running technique.

Deliberate practice demands that you don't get lazy as you train with your team. This is something I see time and again with soccer players. They complete drills with poor body language, in a 'switched off' manner. Stretch yourself. Strive to complete every drill to the best of your ability. Be the best at doing exercises, practices and drills on the team. Execute them with a goal in mind and with complete confidence.

When you play small sided games or practice matches deliver a performance outside of your comfort zone. Play with freedom and focus. Try to do things you haven't done before. Experiment! If the coach asks you to rein things in then do so but until that time look to broaden your set of skills by attempting new movements, new techniques and new plays.

In this way you set a path to becoming an expert performer. You'll start to see things on the pitch differently and see things that you hadn't seen before. And I mean both visually and mentally.

Expert performers in any walk of life have a better and faster understanding of what they see. An expert driver will see a hazardous situation before a novice driver. An expert tennis player will see the way his opponent is shaping up to hit the ball. He can predict where the ball will come back to him and with what type of spin.

Great footballers have this kind of 'better and faster' understanding of the game. The game is slower to them. They have a feel for the game that enables them to make decisions and constant adjustments before everyone else. This starts with deliberate practice. This starts by practicing more and then by making sure you are taxing your brain as you train – stretching yourself.

In your next training session practice playing with
too much confidence

Know a little more

As I mentioned in the introduction to this book the beauty of my profession is that I can help players improve without them having to break sweat. They can work on their mindset in the quiet solitude of their own home.

The great thing about deliberate practice is that it encompasses not only the times you are training but it also involves the notion of studying the game. If you start the process of becoming a student of the game then every minute you spend in learning mode counts toward your 10,000 hours of practice.

Do you understand the formation your coach likes you to play in? Are you aware of the role and responsibilities of your team mates?

You may not be able to play like Xavi Hernandes but do you know as much about playing as a midfielder as he does? You may not score any goals for AC Milan but do you know your striker role as well as Zlatan Ibrahimovic? If not, why not? It's only knowledge, and yet knowledge is a powerful forerunner to skill. When you know more you can do more.

Do you watch much soccer? You probably do, but let me re-phrase this question slightly. Do you study much soccer? When you next settle down to watch one of the world's leading games such as Barcelona versus Real Madrid, Inter Milan versus AC Milan, or Manchester United versus Chelsea I invite you to study the game as you watch. This means taking your eye away from the ball and focusing on the players.

Watch their movement, the runs they make, their touch on the ball and the passes they complete. Specifically study the players in the position you play. Ask yourself

- What are they thinking?
- What are they seeing that helps them make the decisions they make?
- What are they feeling?

Chapter 10

I have asked you several times to imagine yourself as a world beater. It is especially important you exercise your imagination when you watch soccer.

When does the defender I'm watching close down his opposition? What body shape do they keep to be able to see man and ball? When do box-to-box midfielders surge forward and when do they track back? What movement helps the striker I'm watching lose a defender? How is he getting free from his marker inside the box?

Questions, question, questions. Answer these questions in your mind and imagine yourself on the pitch in the game you are watching making the same plays as the world beaters you are learning from.

This works, and works powerfully. How? As a result of a quirk of the brain.

Working harder than the opposition only gets you so far. Working with greater quality should be your aim

Your brain has mirrors

"On your marks."

Everyone in the stadium starts to hush.

"Set."

The silence is painful.

"Bang."

I don't know about you but when I watch top level sport I experience a little of what the competitors do. When I watch the Olympic final of the 100 meters I can feel my body shake a little and I can sense my heart rate jump slightly. I don't have the same nerves as those who are running, but I do get a few nervous sensations running up and down my body.

Emotions and actions are easy to catch. When we see someone cry or laugh, display anger or show pain we can share a piece of what they experience. Equally when we watch a powerful movie filled with emotion our own feelings swell and when we listen to great music by a band - it's as if we can experience a piece of what they are going through.

The secret behind this lies in our brain. Over twenty years ago a group of Italian researchers hooked wires up to the brains of monkeys. They found that the brains responded in the same way whether they were picking up some food or simply watching other monkeys pick up food. The *same* region of the brain would light up. There have been identical results in humans. If I was to watch you switch on the TV, the areas of my brain that would respond would be the same areas that engage if I was turning on the TV myself.

So what has essentially been discovered is that the brain has mirrors. This means we do a lot of our learning by watching other people. This includes sport as well. For example, a scientist called Daniel Glaser asked some ballet dancers to watch other ballet dancers while he hooked up some wires to their brains. He found that the dancers had substantial activity in the part of the brain that controlled dancing when watching other ballet dancers.

It's clear I can watch you do something, such as chipping a football, remember it, then use the same skill later. That sounds obvious but how many of you take time to model players who are better than you or who are better than you in a certain area of the game such as tackling or passing?

The process of learning from others is a genuine part of your 10,000 hours of training. Simply by watching someone play you are feeding your mind and developing your skill.

 Working hard and working with quality despite not feeling at your best. That is mental toughness

Chapter 10

Be position specific

Choose a player to model who plays in the same position as you. As a real world example, Carlton Cole chose to take time watching Didier Drogba and John Carew play. He enjoyed taking DVDs home from the West Ham training ground to watch them play from the comfort of his sofa.

Choose a player whose attributes you'd like to build into your game. If you're a central defender you might like to watch the competitiveness and strength of Carlos Puyol. A full back might clip footage of Paulo Maldini or Ashley Cole. Perhaps as a midfielder you might get inspired by watching old recordings of Zinedine Zidane. Whilst you might not be able to replicate his skills, just by imagining executing his movements you will get a boost of confidence and motivation. Similarly as a striker you might record the runs of Shevchenko, watch the goals of Ruud Van Nistelrooy, or bring out old highlights of Gary Lineker's positioning.

The point is that you choose someone who you believe has the characteristics that your game can build on.

Use their eyes, their heart and their mind

When you watch your models - try to see the world through their eyes. Mentally place yourself in the body of your chosen player. Feel what he feels. Think what he is thinking. Look where he is looking.

Use the whole of your body. If you are modeling the powerful clearance headers of John Terry feel yourself push off the ground, leap high into the air and launch your head onto the ball. Allow yourself to see the ball soar into the sky and bounce down on the half way line. Add an opponent to make your images as authentic as possible. Feel your opponent jump against you – feel him straining to get his head on the ball. But always win the challenge.

Add a sense of character to your images. If it's John Terry then inject your images with reality by sensing a feeling of dominance. If you are watching the German midfielder Mesut Ozil then add a sense of liveliness and confidence. If it's the French striker Karim Benzema you are modeling then enjoy the feeling of strength that he brings to his game. Putting yourself into the boots of American striker Landon Donovan? Then enjoy a feeling of freedom, dynamism and pace.

Of course there is a little guesswork to this process but I really want you to get into the action when you watch your model. Don't be frightened to act as you watch and picture. Stand up and pretend to trap the ball just as your model does. Jump up and win a header just like your model. I want you to literally do it.

Getting the balance

The quantity and quality of your training is a big determinant of your trajectory as a footballer. However, as we shall discuss in the next chapter it is important to add a sense of patience, calm and relaxation into your training and your game. Driving toward perfection is dangerous – therein lies fear and anger.

11

How to Beat Perfectionism

You want to improve your soccer game but I'd like you to be patient. I'd like you to take each training session as an opportunity to improve just a little – perhaps by 0.001%. That's tiny but when you add those small percentages up over time eventually you become a great deal more competent a soccer player than you were before.

Patience, relaxation, trust, belief and calmness are words I often repeat to the young footballers I work with at QPR and at other clubs across Europe. I reinforce these words daily because I know from experience that footballers can be too hard on themselves. They want to win. They want to play at their best and they want to execute their skills perfectly.

This was particularly true of Jimmy, a young soccer player I worked with a few years ago, who was based at a Premiership club in northern England.

At age 15 Jimmy received a professional contract, an incredibly young age to join the paid ranks. But he really was that good. A dynamic young midfielder he was able to spot passes before his peers. He was able to deliver a perfect dead ball and he read the game quicker than his team mates of a similar age.

But in his first year as a youth team scholar Jimmy's progression started to slow. Instead of continuing to develop his skills his technique and tactical understanding remained static. He appeared lazy and lethargic on the pitch and all too often looked to put 50% effort into his training. This reflected in matches and a series of poor performances had coaching staff seriously concerned about his future.

Why was this happening to Jimmy? He was still the friendly, intelligent young soccer player he had always been. On his day he could still play better than just about anyone else in his age group at the club. And he still wanted with all his heart to be a professional player. But his dead cert career was looking fragile. I had a theory – Jimmy was a perfectionist.

Perfectionism: Your best friend and your worst enemy

We all want to play the perfect game. Whether on the court, the course or the pitch we want our game to look great, to show off in front of our friends, peers and coaches. As a soccer psychology consultant I have worked with hundreds of players who work their backsides to the bone to play the perfect game.

I'm sure that whenever you run onto a football pitch you want to make all your passes, you want to own and dominate the opposition, you want to nail every tackle and you want to win every match six nil.

This kind of attitude is admirable. It sounds like the mindset of a winner – a player with great soccer psychology. And indeed perfectionism in soccer can often be your best friend. It can help drive you to train harder, in all weathers and on all pitch conditions. It can help motivate your mind and can develop a game guided by passion and desire. Someone regarded as a perfectionist may set high standards tough to attain goals and may dream big. He may push himself further. It's fair to say that many of the world's great players have a hint of perfectionism about their attitude and character.

But an attitude of perfectionism can be destructive. It can cause players to get overly angry and frustrated. It can lead to arguments with team mates. It can inject fear into a mindset. And it can cause players to simply give up. Perfectionists rarely perform to their abilities because they're afraid of failing or making the mistakes that will prevent them from winning. These are often the footballers who want to win the most and players who train the hardest, but rarely meet their potential on game day.

Those perfectionists who tend to get angry at themselves on the pitch are often ones who go into a game with expectations that are too high. They say to themselves "*I'm going to score a hat-trick today*" and when, at half time, they haven't scored they start to get angry, stop focusing correctly and start losing confidence. Alternatively, perfectionists may say to themselves "*I'm going to keep a clean sheet today*" and when they go a goal down they lose their focus and their confidence starts to disappear.

Some perfectionists may take things out on their team mates. If their team goes a goal down they create a blame culture by pointing at the person whose mistake may have led to the goal. It's not that they constantly avoid blaming themselves, it's just that they have little or no forgiveness for those who have stopped their team from playing the perfect game. They tend to be poor team mates - willing to castigate first before helping another overcome a moment of poor play or a mistake.

Those perfectionists who tend to play with fear do so because they don't want to make mistakes. They don't want to take risks. They want to avoid looking stupid. Why take risks when perfectionism requires you complete every pass perfectly? The perfectionist passes backwards and sideways, not just once or twice but nearly always.

I often hear players in the changing room before the game boasting that their goal in the game is to complete every pass they make. Therein lays the perfectionist. What a terrible goal to set yourself. So you're not going to try and play the killer ball? You're not going to try and weight a tough through ball for your striker to latch onto?

The perfectionist quickly becomes wracked with fear. He may hide behind the opposition so as not to make himself available for the pass - not showing for it. A perfectionist often gives up – why keep playing when a perfect game has already been destroyed by the terrible pass you gave away in the first minute? Perfectionists so often call time on their game prematurely, before the final whistle has blown.

Having watched Jimmy in a number of training sessions and matches my theory was that he displayed a number of perfectionist tendencies.

Chapter 11

*Striving for perfection in a match is
the enemy of freedom*

Jimmy and the perfect fix

For the most part, my work consists not of a never ending stream of techniques and tools but of conversation. I enjoy nothing more than sitting down with a soccer player and discussing the concepts I talk about in this book. And I use the word concepts because I believe that a lot of my work is more like a series of performance philosophies than just a bunch of techniques.

This was never truer than when trying to get to grips with Jimmy's challenges. As a very intelligent young man Jimmy was (and still is) always questioning. Not for him to just play football and keep quiet. He wants to learn all he can and he has never been afraid to use his voice to ask coaching questions.

When Jimmy and I sat down to talk I put it bluntly to him that I felt he had a perfectionist mindset. I surprised him by congratulating him. I told him that some of the greatest sports competitors of all time have suffered from such an affliction and that if he embarked on making a subtle shift in thinking he'd get himself back on track to playing winning football again.

I told Jimmy I felt he wanted first team soccer so badly that this focus was stifling his progression and performances. I told him it was the cause of his perfectionist attitude. If he didn't play perfectly then he simply didn't feel he was good enough to progress to the first team. If the youth team lost he felt the first team coaches wouldn't want to progress anyone from the youth team.

Jimmy was also having doubts. He feared wasting chances to score, giving the ball away and getting sent off. He played with an acute self-consciousness when the first team coaches came to watch him play and when he got injured he was scared to train until he was completely convinced he was fully fit for fear of re-injuring himself. He was obsessing about having a game good enough for Premiership football, about the future, and he was panicking.

The result was a great young player who played with a hint of fear, a little tentatively, and who played to avoid mistakes rather than to play with confidence. Jimmy wanted to win and to succeed so badly that he was getting in his own way.

He had to step back, enjoy the process of improving, and play with greater freedom.

A pinch of perfectionism is fine. But anymore can lead to anxiety, fear and doubt

Your mindset

Do you find yourself getting angry at yourself for missing gilt edged chances or making a mistake that leads to a goal against your team? Do you find yourself going into a funk as you play, feeling sorry for yourself when the chips are down?

I know that many of you reading this will play in a perfectionist mode because I know how much soccer players love to win. That's one of the reasons you play right? It sounds crazy but an obsession to win comes wrapped in a package of worry, doubt, fear and anger. Rather than playing with a mindset focused on your script - your focus of attention can be on the quality of your technique. You may over-analyze your performances. And you may do this as you play.

A real hallmark of the perfectionist is underperformance in matches. If you train really well but tend to play in matches with inconsistency then you may have a perfectionist mindset.

It is the repetition of the basics that makes the complex look simple

Chapter 11

The 3 F's: focus, fun and freedom

Jimmy was excited and I hope you are too. My 3 F's drill not only helps the perfectionist, but also any soccer player wishing to play with a more consistent mindset. I'd go as far to say that if you execute the 3 F's correctly in every game you will play with quality every single time. That's a bold statement I know, but one I'm willing to make.

The first stage of the 3 F's is Focus. And quite simply this refers to creating, thinking about and focusing on the Script I introduced you to in Chapter 6 - as you play. Combating a perfectionist mindset is made much easier by having plays that you can control - to focus on - as you compete. The Script takes your mind away from winning and from the mistakes you've made during the game. It also sustains your effort and energy levels if you start to feel like giving up.

The next 2 stages in the 3 F's go hand in hand. They are Fun and Freedom.

I want all my clients to have fun on the pitch no matter what their ambition in the game is. The term 'fun' may be a bit wishy-washy but to me if you pair it with the term freedom you will have a more concrete idea of the style of play I'm talking about. Let's do a little exercise:

Take a few minutes to build the scene in your mind.

You are on the pitch, you are having fun and you are playing with complete unadulterated freedom. You are loose, you are free, you are fearless.

- What does this look and feel like?
- What does it look and feel like in the air, in the tackle, and with your movement?
- What is your body language like? How loud and vocal are you?
- What are you like in your role and with your responsibilities?

Be very clear in your mind - what does fun and freedom look and feel like? Blow it up - make it big, bold and bright. Done that? Great! Now do it every day.

And I don't want you to stop there. I want you to take those feelings and sensations into training with you. I want you playing with fun and freedom. And the crucial thing here in training - the most important thing that must become a habit and a pattern - is that you mustn't let anything or anyone take you away from these feelings of fun and freedom. You dictate your attitude on the pitch -

not the opposition, not the weather, and not the state of the pitch. Only you dictate your ability to play with fun and freedom.

On match day go out and deliver a performance full of the 3 F's. Play with focus, fun, and freedom. Play in tune with the 3 F's for 90 minutes. Let nothing and no-one take you away from this mindset. If you go a goal down, stick to your 3 F's. If you make a mistake, stick to your 3 F's. If a team mate slips and hands the opposition a goal, stick to your 3 F's.

In fact I'd go as far to say that all you can expect from yourself on the pitch is to focus on the plays in your Script, to have fun and to play with freedom. Stop expecting to win, to lose, to score or to concede. You are a competitor and not a supporter nor a gambler. Direct your expectations onto executing your 3 F's as best you can. By doing so - you will play at your best.

My philosophies to combat perfectionism

Over the course of quite a few sessions Jimmy and I engaged in conversation revolving around some of my playing philosophies. Here are a few about playing with perfection:

- A footballer who constantly strives for perfection has to understand that football is a game of imperfection. It is too hard a game to get everything right and a big part of being human is getting things wrong. Pele didn't play perfectly. Nor did Maradona. Lionel Messi doesn't play with perfection every match. Nor did Bobby Moore. A footballer has to love this fact as much as he loves the game itself. Enjoy the imperfections of the game – the bad bounces, the mistakes from you and from team mates, and the refereeing decisions that go against you.

- A footballer has to understand that technical perfection is an impossible dream. You will spill the ball from time to time, strike it poorly, play a poorly weighted or misdirected pass, and deliver a lousy corner. You have over 300 bones in your body. You're not going to co-ordinate them perfectly all the time. Relax – perfectionism is only going to make your body tighter and ruin your technique anyway.

- A football player has to understand that perfectionism constricts her play, her creativity, and her decision making. Your mind and body works best when you allow yourself to play, to move and to think with a mindset dedicated to fun and freedom. Playing freely enables you to take the necessary risks to play the ball that sets up winning goals, that helps a team mate to make runs behind the defense and enables her to reach for awkward crossing balls. Play with a mindset of trust. Call this your trusting mode. In your trusting mode you don't beat yourself up or fear the consequences of failure. You simply play in accordance to the plays in your Script. In your trusting mode you know that the training you have completed will be enough to make winning passes and winning tackles. You know that the training and practice you've put in means you can allow your technique to flow without over-thinking your bodily movement.

- A soccer player has to understand that with perfectionism comes anger and fear and that these are not the route to excellence. Playing with focus and leaving mistakes behind (as we shall discover in the next section of this book) will help him become the most effective and consistent footballer he can be.

- A soccer player should strive to win but not at the expense of playing without focus and confidence. Playing with these two mindset qualities permits you to play in the zone. Forcing the result doesn't. Perfectionism is anti-zone. It is filled with anger, fear and with individualism. Believe you can win, but don't expect to win. Believe you can win but avoid thinking about winning while you play. Believe you can win but focus your mind tightly on the present moment as each second ticks by.

Ultimately all you can do is....

Play with fun and freedom and focus on executing your script. If there is a secret to performance it is this. Champions don't *force* themselves to win or to play with perfection. They know they *can't* control winning and they know they *can't* compete with perfection. If there is a fallacy about performance it is the idea of 'making things happen'. If anything, under pressure, the world's greatest sports competitors relax and allow things to happen. If they make a mistake they may turn up the volume of their focus or relax even more (to break away from tension) but they don't force the process of performance.

Relax, be calm, show patience. Your performance will take care of itself. Just absorb your mind in fun, freedom and your Script.

12

How Batman Grew

I'd never seen pace like it.

Batman pushed the ball forward with the inside of his foot. It looked too far and too easy for the defenders to chase down. But Batman had other ideas, or at least the rockets in his feet did. Giving the two opposing defenders a 5 yard head start Batman proceeded to run past them, control the ball, then play a pinpoint perfect cross for the striker to nestle the ball in the back of the net.

Sitting in the stands I wondered what this young footballer was doing playing in the Blue Square South division (England's division 6). His pace was electric. The first 10 meters covered with speed, the first touch on the ball controlled, the final ball delivered accurately into the danger zone. He was surely a little too good for this level.

But this was a pre-season game. This was a game with no pressure – a warm up match with players feeling their way into the team. It wasn't until a few games into the season that Batman's challenges unfolded. He could be very good. He just had to believe that it was *possible* for him to be very good.

Chapter 12

The Batman: the story of Shaun Batt

Fisher Athletic's Manager Wayne Burnett had established an exciting squad. With an average age of 21, it was packed with players who had just failed to make the grade at league level. Young, ambitious and full of hope – the season promised to be exciting.

Shaun Batt (known by fans as Batman) was one of those players. He was only in his early twenties but stints at Stevenage Borough and Dagenham and Redbridge hadn't panned out as he'd expected - so he decided to try his luck a few levels lower with Fisher in the Blue Square South. He knew playing under Burnett would suit his game. The young manager liked to play quick, tidy soccer keeping the ball on the ground with a passing game other teams would envy.

And excitement was rife when Fisher held the top of the table after three games with three wins. Shaun had played in all the games and had played okay without displaying the brilliance of pre-season. He still showed lightening pace but occasionally his touch was off, and sometimes a cross into the penalty box lacked flight or over-shot the area.

Small inconsistencies continued to plague his game. He wasn't off by much and he was a constant starter for Fisher but with the team dropping down the table his form was occasionally sensational and sometimes not at the level he wanted. We chatted now and again on the team bus, and after training, and it was during our conversations that it dawned on me that the potential I and others saw in Batman wasn't necessarily the potential he saw in himself. I had an inkling that his inconsistencies of performance stemmed from a fixed mindset.

 It is your inner comfort zone that holds you back

Growth versus fixed mindset

One of the most important names in psychology right now is a woman called Carol Dweck. She is a psychologist at Stanford University in California. She has worked on a project she calls *Mindset* which places people into one of two categories – those with a fixed mindset and those with a growth mindset.

In a fixed mindset, people believe their basic attributes and characteristics - like their intelligence or their talent - are fixed. They believe that what you become is a result of inborn ability. These people believe they have a certain level of talent and nothing can or will change that.

In a growth mindset, people believe that their most basic abilities can be developed through dedication and hard work - talent is just their starting point. If they have talent then they're happy, but they don't see this talent as the thing that will get them where they want to go.

As a footballer one of the most important qualities you must possess is to believe in the growth mindset. Do you?

If you think your skills are set in stone then I'd argue that you don't have a growth mindset. If you look at a team mate or a member of another team and believe that you can never get as good as that player then it's likely you have a fixed mindset. If your inner voice tends to say "*I am who I am*" then I'd propose that you are not of a growth mindset.

In the early part of the season I spent with Fisher Athletic I felt that Shaun Batt was being held back by a fixed mindset. I felt that not only was he a lot better than he gave himself credit for, but that he didn't believe he had it inside of him to be a League player. I got the impression Shaun felt you were or you weren't, you had it or you hadn't.

I wanted some belief, some fire from Shaun. I wanted him to stop limiting his horizons. I believed that doing so pushed him into a world of inconsistent performances. Shaun had to learn to grow. He had to trust that the best are the best because they work harder than everyone else and believe they can get to the very top.

Actions can become habits and so can thought.
Make both your actions & thoughts awesome!

Maradona, Messi, and other greats

Diego Maradona, Lionel Messi, and other soccer players like Pele, Mia Hamm, Ronaldo and Zinedine Zidane were all gifted. They all had talent and ability. It only takes a couple of minutes to look on YouTube to see a young Maradona do keepie-uppies and a pre-teen Lionel Messi dance his way through a group of soccer players to score 8, 9, and 10 goals a game.

We probably can't all be as good as these players but we can certainly explore becoming a better footballer, no matter how good that is. No-one has a monopoly on telling you what you can and can't do. If you play fun 5-a-side games but you have a dream and desire to play for County or State teams then start to do the things that will help you to grow as a footballer.

A part of being Soccer Tough is not letting anyone decide your soccer future for you. It is only your voice you should listen to. It is for *you* to tell *you* how good *you* can be. Don't allow anyone's negative voice to carry with you onto the training or match day pitch. Keep talking to yourself positively. Maintain a 'can do' growth mindset.

The ability to play positively under pressure
doesn't happen overnight. It is a result of thinking
correctly for 100's of training sessions

Gianfranco Zola

My days working with Carlton Cole allowed me to see some of the most enjoyable training sessions you could ever wish to see. I got to watch the brilliant Italian soccer player Gianfranco Zola in action. Zola was on his very first managerial role but was young enough and fit enough to join in with training. I wasn't alone in thinking that the manager in his early 40s was the best player on the training pitch at that time regularly eclipsing the younger players.

Zola played at Italian club Napoli during his early years, a club that was one of the best in Europe at the time. They had some of the world's greatest players including Brazilians Careca and Alamoa, and one Diego Maradona. Zola said this about the Argentinian:

"When I first met him I was only 23 and just a young player trying to get better and I had him in front of me. The best player in the world, so I felt lucky. When you have that it inspires you to do better and it was a challenge to get my level of football to his. I used to stay longer on the training ground with him, trying free-kicks and playing small games."

In fact they practiced together for hours. While others went inside to shower and change - Diego Maradona and Gianfranco Zola enjoyed several hours of working on the flight of their free kicks, the weight of their passes, touch, ball control and the accuracy of their shot.

Picture in your mind: Zola watching Diego Maradona line up a free kick. His eyes fixed attentively on the body and feet of the great man. What did he see? What vision penetrated the mind of Zola? Maradona wrapping his boot around the side of the ball, sending it curving on the perfect trajectory just inside the top corner.

Picture Zola playing one-versus-one against Maradona – learning how to read the slight body movements that allowed Maradona to float around players as if they weren't there. Zola's mind would have picked up on these, his mirror neurons working overtime. Maradona leans left then right, Zola equal to the moves of the master. Maradona constantly taunting his younger opponent, unremitting in his play. Zola stretched left then right, brain in perpetual thinking mode, legs working non-stop, heart growing stronger all the time.

Gianfranco Zola and Diego Maradona – 10,000 hours in action and the masters of deliberate practice.

Both born brilliant soccer players? Maybe! They both had a physical gift that's for sure. But what is without dispute is that both worked as hard as or harder than other footballers around the world. Both were completely committed to their soccer growth.

The brain changes with every minute of every day.
Can you optimize your life to help your brain
change in the best way possible

Your Brain

During my season with Fisher Athletic I spent time with every member of the team teaching them a little bit about the brain and how it develops. I wanted them to understand that 'you are your brain' and that your brain is something that can grow and develop every day of your life.

Indeed, everything you do and everything you say in life is driven by your brain, specifically by the billions of tiny connections (called synapses) in your brain. Each time we learn something new we activate different brain cells and create new connections between cells. Essentially learning a new move in football means you connect up a new bunch of brain cells – your brain changes its structure.

This process gets to the heart of growth. What we now know in brain science is that the brain can continue to establish new connections (and learn) for the whole of your life. Yes it's easier to learn when you're younger but it's still very possible to keep learning throughout the whole of adulthood.

If you play in a mid-age soccer team and you want to improve your skills and your mindset - you can. You can because science has shown you can. Anyone can grow their football no matter what age they are and no matter what level they play at. The limits you put on your game are your own restrictions. I want my clients to be no-limit soccer players. I want them to dream about and then take action on being quicker, stronger and more effective on the pitch. I want them to work on delivering better movement, an increased range of passing and more powerful shots.

*The brain is like a muscle. It can be
exercised, trained and nurtured just
like any other part of the body*

Shaun's Solutions

I told Shaun Batt, just as I would tell you, that you have a computer system that
you carry around with you every day that automatically changes from moment to
moment. It's your brain. And there is no limit as to how powerful this system can
become. Its power is determined by the conscious inputs (your thoughts) you
install daily. And these inputs are a choice – you can choose to make them
positive and helpful so your system's power increases.

You also have a choice as to how your system changes. You can choose to wire it
in a way that improves your skills or you can choose to wire it in a way that
diminishes your abilities. You get a choice through the medium of thinking, by
the direction of your focus on and off the pitch, as well as through the quantity
and quality of your practice.

Shaun Batt went on to score many goals that season and help Fisher finish fourth
with a group of young players in a division that demands strength, power and
experience. He did this partly because he had great ability but also because he
started to believe in this ability and started to understand that he could still build
on his physical gifts. As a result of his great season Shaun won a contract with a
League One side and four years on is now contracted to a Championship club.

Can anyone achieve anything with a growth mindset? Of course not! Batman may
never play Champions League football or represent his country in the World Cup
- but Batman will become *the very best soccer player he can be* if he believes he
can get to that level. And if he continues to take this approach, who knows... He
should never let anyone tell him otherwise.

As a great French Philosopher once wrote *"It is our duty as men and women to
proceed as though the limits of our abilities do not exist."* It is your duty as a

Chapter 12

soccer player to do so and it is your duty as a football coach to help your players do so. The next chapter will introduce you to someone who, despite tough times, has continued to learn, develop and grow.

13

Adding Mind to Barry's Heart

It was my friend Josh Wright who delivered the corner.

His perfect in-swinger was met by the head of striker Simeon Jackson. The ball hit the back of the net before the keeper could see it. The Gillingham FC fans went mad - a last minute goal with no time for the opposition to come back. The club was about to win the 2009 English League 2 play-offs.

As the fans celebrated they wouldn't have noticed captain of the club Barry Fuller back on the halfway line taking everything in. He wanted to celebrate with his team mates but he knew there would be a few minutes of injury time to play, so he made sure he remained composed. At the same time he couldn't help but inwardly smile at the way things were unfolding for him. Barry's life hadn't just been a rollercoaster, his ride had nearly come to an end just five months earlier.

In January 2009 Barry Fuller lay in a hospital bed semi-conscious suffering with pneumonia. His family, beside themselves with grief, were by his bed praying every day for him to recover. For 7 days he lay there unable to speak, his breathing aided by an oxygen mask, his body malnourished and decimated by illness.

His team mates visited and concerned coaches planned for a season without Barry. Yet just over four weeks later he played against Rotherham United in a league match. Barry is certainly brave.

Barry's story

I met Barry Fuller when giving a soccer psychology presentation to the Gillingham team. I wouldn't call Barry a client but we share the same positive philosophies after my visit sparked his interest for the mental side of soccer.

Barry's story is one to capture the imagination. Released by Charlton at the age of 22 he joined non-league side Barnet and then played a few seasons at Stevenage before joining his current club Gillingham. He would admit to being more warrior than artist – flair play was never his thing. But for sheer will and want on the pitch then Barry is your man.

He didn't even have to think about giving it his all. It just came naturally to him. His inner voice on the pitch would drive him to keep going for 90 minutes, especially in that last lung-busting 5 minutes. He was great at inspiring team mates and his positive body language helped him play at an intensity the game demands.

But having a never-say-die attitude on the pitch isn't always backed up with positive and helpful thinking off it. And it took his near fatal illness, combined with my visit to Gillingham, for Barry to start exploring his thought processes. Barry was ready to grow.

Barry's soccer growth

My visit to Gillingham got Barry thinking. Was he really that positive a person? Did he really spend time every day proactively thinking about playing at his best? Was he directing his thinking or was his thinking directing him? Was he setting goals for his training sessions? Was he actively partaking in deliberate practice?

To grow you have to ask yourself these same questions. You have to get to the heart of your development as a footballer. You have to be honest with yourself. Are you giving yourself the best opportunity to succeed in your football?

Do you have success seeking habits in place every day?

Are you examining the areas that need to improve in your game and developing a program to improve them?

Are you consistent with the quality of your training in every session?

Answer these questions honestly. If your response to any of them is *no* then you're not giving yourself the best chance to be the best soccer player you can be. You're not stretching your mind and body.

Barry decided things had to change. He was happy with his mindset when he took to the pitch but believed he could feel a little more confident going into games. I had taken the Gillingham players through the process of developing a match Script so he started to do that at the beginning of each week.

Barry would set aside a little time each day to re-read the match plays he had chosen for his script, and to picture executing them as vividly as his imagination allowed. Just opening up a few images in his mind enabled him to gain greater clarity of the responsibilities he had on match day, and boosted his confidence for the upcoming game.

Are you writing out a match script yet? Are you taking time to picture your match script every day? Have you committed to executing your match script when you get the chance in training?

Barry also decided to be more proactive with his thinking. He read as many books on effective thinking as he could find. He read articles on some of the greatest sports competitors the world has ever seen. He would regularly jot down passages from these books which helped him have a more positive outlook. His wife got involved and sent him text messages of motivational quotes to keep his thoughts pointing in the right direction – toward success.

A future champion is a fortune teller. He can clearly see his future...that's why he becomes a champion

Being inspired

Barry Fuller is a big boxing fan. Although he is a professional in a team sport he appreciates the art and science of competing in an individual sport. He understands how durable you have to be to self-motivate without a group of team mates around you - others to keep you working and to keep you focused when you just don't fancy putting in the training hours. Barry points to boxing as the ultimate in mental toughness: *"To even consider getting in that ring,"* he said, *"you have to have an enormously positive outlook. You can't even consider defeat."*

To this end Barry is fascinated by the confidence a boxer has, and he has spent time trying to adopt the same inner voice that greats such as Floyd Mayweather and a true hero of his - Muhammad Ali - have. Don't misunderstand me. Barry doesn't walk around telling everyone how great he is, but through his study into the art of positive psychology he now understands that how he speaks to himself influences how he feels which subsequently determines how he performs. He wants to feel great so he works on talking to himself in a way that helps him feel that way.

I don't always like the way some boxers behave, although the cynic in me does wonder if they are just trying to sell tickets for their shows. But I do share with Barry his love of the way boxers go about the mentality of their trade. The boxer is uncompromising with his inner voice.

No one talked to themselves better than the great Muhammad Ali. Here are a few of his historic quotes:

"I am the greatest; I said that even before I knew I was."

"I hated every minute of training, but I said, "Don't quit. Suffer now and live the rest of your life as a champion." "

"It's lack of faith that makes people afraid of meeting challenges, and I believed in myself."

"It's the repetition of affirmations that leads to belief. And once that belief becomes a deep conviction, things begin to happen."

You can't help but be inspired can you? You can't help but think big when you listen to this iconic figure. He has dozens of quotes pretty much saying the same thing *"I talk to myself confidently time and again"*.

Was he scared going into the ring in his famous bouts against Sonny Liston and George Foreman? Of course he was. But he refused to listen to that inner voice of doubt. Did he have some doubts? Probably! But what Ali intuitively understood was that the more he talked to himself in a confident, upbeat, and energized manner the better he'd feel about himself, the more confident he'd be, and the better he'd perform.

Do you have a Muhammad Ali voice inside of you? If you want to improve your soccer - having one will help. I'm not talking about adopting an outward portrayal of arrogance. I don't have time for that on the football pitch. I'm talking about an inner voice of confidence and growth. Football is an extremely competitive game and if you want to play with all your heart, with maximum strength, and with extreme durability - you need self-talk that narrates a tale of '*I can do*' and '*I will do*'.

This is my pitch, this is my game. I own my position. There is nothing and no-one to take me away from a confident and focused mindset.

I am the best in training every single time. I never compromise my training mentality. I'm first in sprints, my movement is unbelievable in small sided games, and my voice is the loudest on the pitch.

I compete with quality every time I step foot on a pitch. I'm intelligent – aware, alert, alive and I deliver a performance of the highest caliber every single time.

No one can touch me off the ball. No one gets near my ability to see what is going on around me, to read the play 10 seconds ahead, and to anticipate the opposition's next move.

I want your inner voice related to your soccer to mirror the confidence of the finest sports people on the planet. You may not be the best ever soccer player but no one can take your inner voice away from you. No one can stop you enjoying the inner movies of a champion. They are yours to experience and to keep.

Be inspired. Take time to read articles on great sportsmen and women. Adopt an inner voice like theirs. Use this voice at home and take it out onto the training pitch. Carry it with you on match day. Let it be your natural way of speaking to yourself.

Every word you say to yourself deposits confidence or fear...toward or away from your goals and dream

Chapter 13

Setback versus growth

Not every soccer journey is straightforward. Especially Barry's. At the end of the 2010/11 season Barry was involved in a collision with another player in a game against Macclesfield FC. Hobbling off he thought he'd just bruised his knee. But it felt painful and he asked to be examined further.

Initial tests came back quite positive; as he'd expected - just severe bruising and he played on for the remainder of the season. But by the start of the 2011/12 season Barry still felt pain in his knee and the club sent him to a knee specialist. What the specialist discovered was alarming. Barry had snapped a part of the posterolateral corner of his knee. He proceeded to have career threatening surgery and sit on the sidelines for nine months.

It was during these nine months that the soccer growth program that Barry was committed to really paid off. His inner voice told him quietly that his career was over but he shouted back *"No, it's going to be ok. I'm going to play again. I'm going to reach my targets"*.

Watch a duck paddle across a pond and what you see is a serene looking bird swimming with ease. But underneath the water's surface the duck is kicking its legs at a rapid rate to get from point a to point b. This is an image I get a lot of clients to envisage. I want them to understand the picture of the duck swimming is a lot like the process of dealing with negative self-talk. On the outside everything appears normal but on the inside your inner voice is trying hard to stay positive and upbeat.

This was the internal battle that Barry continued to have during his enforced lay off. His negative voice was ever present and he had to persist in breaking it by reinforcing the positive, having a 'can do' attitude, and creating pictures of future success. He had to take charge of his thinking so he could continue to feel belief in himself as a footballer.

Win any internal battle you are having with fear and worry and doubt. Put negativity to the sword by releasing 'can do' pictures into your mind. Walk as if you are the best, talk to yourself as if you are the best. Yes of course there will be times when the voice of negativity is loud but you now have the tools and techniques to squash any unhelpful thoughts.

Winning happens in the mind first. If you don't see yourself as a winner then you need to take a hold of your thoughts

The commitment you need

You may think that by simply reading this book you will grow your soccer game. That's a nice thought but you would be sadly mistaken. Growing your soccer game is an everyday thing. It's an every training session thing, and an every match thing. It must be done through patience, perseverance and practice.

Barry Fuller is committed to his growth. He doesn't know the level he'll reach by the end of his career but he has high expectations of himself. He expects to improve his thinking every day. He knows this will deliver a high level of self-belief and bullet proof confidence going into matches. Does this mean he'll never make a mistake on the pitch again? Of course not. But he has a match Script to deal with that eventuality.

Barry certainly doesn't want to get injured again. But he knows 'stuff happens'. He knows a 'hammy' or a tear of some sort may be around the corner but he knows that his football growth program will once again help him through any tough times ahead.

A great footballer works hard on managing his thinking both on and off the pitch

At the time of writing this book Barry is looking forward to the 2012/13 season. He has retained his playing rights at Gillingham and will possibly retain captaincy of the club in the new season despite his prolonged absence. He sees the last nine months, not as a time of loss but as a blessed time of opportunity. He has exercised his soccer growth program to its full capacity and has given himself a mindset that will stand him in good stead as he progresses onto the second half of his career.

To my mind Barry is an example of a footballer who was open minded enough to realize that despite the mental toughness he has always had - he could become mentally *stronger*. I think that is a quality all footballers need. Never give up on progression. Always have a growth mindset. It's something I try to instill in my youngest clients, in fact all of my clients. I hope they continue to learn to grow. I hope they continue to develop their mindset. I hope they continue to love their soccer journey.

Full-time

Your soccer image guides the belief you have as a soccer player. Your self-belief determines your performance confidence and subsequently drives how you perform under the lights on match day. But it starts with your soccer image so make your image great... make it exciting and exceptional!

A champion footballer is a master thinker. He fills the image he has of himself as a competitor with positive, helpful and constructive thoughts. He knows his mindset is a choice and he enjoys opening up a catalogue of pictures that embodies his best. He is familiar with this inner movie and comfortable making these pictures big and bold and bright.

Remember to remember – memory brings bubbles of excellence to the surface. A champion uses the resources of the past. He takes time to envision his best games and his best moments. He does this every day without fail.

A champion footballer imagines. He dares to dream of accomplishment. He predicts success. His questions deliver inner sketches of his next match that builds his soccer image and injects his confidence.

Remember to predict – use your imagination. Imagine a soccer world yet to come. Your next match is going to be your dream game – what does this look and feel like? Build your performance fuel as you approach a match by daring to envision excellence.

Full-time

A champion footballer manages his thinking in the moment. He experiences failure yet he puts these episodes to good use. He feeds his mindset pictures of his strengths to build self-belief while allowing thoughts of weaknesses to encourage him to improve every component of his game

Remember to perceive positively – perception manages fear before it strikes. Never be a slave to events – your mind must shape how you see everything that happens to you on and off the pitch.

A champion controls the controllables. He knows what he can manage and what must be ignored. He performs with a focus on his game, with a mindset on the present moment and with specific, tangible processes to execute.

Remember to write your script – your preparation must include setting plays to think about, and to focus on, when you perform. A mental game plan! Come back to your script when you are distracted. Stick to your script when you are losing. Stick to your script when you are winning. Stay in the me, the now, the script.

A champion uses his inner voice and his body language to climb into the zone – to stay zoned. He energises himself, he relaxes himself – both through the process of self-management. He notices when he's thinking negatively and cuts this way of thinking immediately.

Remember to squash your ANTs - let nothing and no-one take you away from your high performance mindset. Allow your confidence and focus to rise – to soar – by spotting and stopping unhelpful, negative thoughts. Get on your toes – be alert, alive, ready for everything that the opposition throw at you.

A champion develops his game by executing success seeking habits every day without fail. That is his commitment to the process of improvement – he knows there is no day off, no break from doing, being and thinking.

Remember to train hard and to train with quality. Your 10,000 hour journey must be accompanied by effective methods of practice. Immerse yourself in the process of improvement by engaging in deliberate practice. Be a student of the game. Repeat things, stretch yourself and garner feedback from others. It may not be fun but it is your route to distinction.

When you play - compete with psychology in mind. When you analyse your game - scrutinise with psychology in mind. When you think about building your future game do so with psychology in mind.

Be a champion on the pitch. If pressure bears down on you play to win and not to lose. Play on the front foot and not the back foot. Play with freedom and not with fear. Remove the burden of pressure by climbing onto your toes. Get your head up to survey the pitch – awareness settles your nerves. Enjoy a sense of fun and liberate your feet by allowing them to dance. Add a pinch of focus to your mindset but let it settle on the plays in your script. Slow if you must – speed up if necessary. The body and mind are the twin joysticks for your performance intensity.

When you take to the pitch there are your team mates and there is your opposition but the playing surface is yours – *you* own it. *You* will determine how you will play, no one else. That is the belief you need, the inner voice you need, the confidence you need.

Never be too up or too down as a consequence of your soccer matches. A champion's mind stays firmly on course to grow no matter his team's results. If you win it's time to improve. If you lose it's time to improve. If you are man of the match it's time to improve. Commit to your football growth through good times and bad. That is the mindset you need. That is Soccer Tough.

Graduation: Life Lessons of a Professional Footballer by Richard Lee

The 2010/11 season will go down as a memorable one for Goalkeeper Richard Lee. Cup wins, penalty saves, hypnotherapy and injury would follow, but these things only tell a small part of the tale. Filled with anecdotes, insights, humour and honesty - Graduation uncovers Richard's campaign to take back the number one spot, save a lot of penalties, and overcome new challenges. What we see is a transformation - beautifully encapsulated in this extraordinary season.

"Whatever level you have played the beautiful game and whether a goalkeeper or outfield player, you will connect with this book. Richard's honesty exposes the fragility in us all, he gives an honest insight into dimensions of a footballer's life that are often kept a secret and in doing so offers worthy advice on how to overcome any hurdle. A great read." **Ben Foster, Goalkeeper, West Bromwich Albion.**

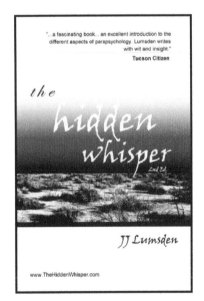

The Hidden Whisper by Dr JJ Lumsden

Want to learn about the science of parapsychology and paranormal phenomena? Follow the exploits of fictional parapsychologist Dr Luke Jackson as he seeks to uncover a poltergeist outbreak in Southern Arizona. Along the way, learn all about paranormal phenomena such as Extra Sensory Perception, Psychokinesis, Ghosts, Poltergeists, Out of Body Experiences and more.

This book works on many levels, an excellent introduction to the concepts current in the field of parapsychology... at best you may learn something new, and at worst you'll have read a witty and well-written paranormal detective story. **Parascience**

...a ghost investigation novel that has all the elements of a good detective mystery and spooky thriller...an engrossing haunting tale... an informative overview of the current theories on the phenomena. **paranormal.about.com**

An extremely well-written and suspenseful page-turner from real life parapsychologist JJ Lumsden. **Yoga Magazine**

Around the World in 80 Scams: an Essential Travel Guide by Peter John

Every year, thousands of people fall victim to various travel scams, crimes and confidence tricks while they travel. Most people escape having simply lost a little money, but many lose much more, and some encounter real personal danger

This essential book is a practical, focused, and detailed guide to eighty of the most common scams and crimes travellers might encounter. It is packed with real-world examples drawn from resources across the globe and the author's own travels. Being aware of scammers' tricks is the best way of avoiding them altogether.

Chapters cover all sorts of scams including: Hotels and other accommodation scams, Transport scams, Eating, drinking and gambling scams, Begging and street hustling scams, Extortion, blackmail and fraud scams, and more.

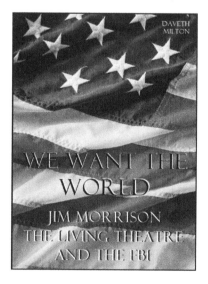

We Want The World: Jim Morrison, The Living Theatre and the FBI by Daveth Milton

Jim Morrison was a songwriter, film maker, poet and singer with The Doors. His opponents saw him as a criminal. And more. In an escalating confrontation over the freedom of America, he was up against men who used law to block justice and fear to halt social change. Those men included the FBI's infamous director, J. Edgar Hoover.

Inspired by true events, this imaginative recreation of history re-opens Morrison's secret FBI dossier to reveal his Establishment opponents. Moving between Jim's image, influences and brushes with the law in Phoenix and Miami, Daveth Milton uses meticulous research skills to assess the extent of the conspiracy against the singer. Part meditation, part rock in the dock exposé, We Want The World provides the ultimate account of Jim Morrison's awkward encounter with the Bureau.

Lightning Source UK Ltd.
Milton Keynes UK
UKOW07f1949290216

269335UK00004B/167/P